T0279611

HUMILITY

The Secret History of a Lost Virtue

HUMILITY

The Secret History of a Lost Virtue

CHRISTOPHER M. BELLITTO

Georgetown University Press / Washington, DC

The publisher is not responsible for third-party websites or their content.
URL links were active at time of publication.

Library of Congress Cataloging-in-Publication Data

Names: Bellitto, Christopher M., author.
Title: Humility : the secret history of a lost virtue / Christopher M. Bellitto.
Description: Washington, DC : Georgetown University Press, 2023. |
Includes bibliographical references and index.
Identifiers: LCCN 2022051977 (print) | LCCN 2022051978 (ebook) |
ISBN 9781647123765 (hardcover) | ISBN 9781647123772 (ebook)
Subjects: LCSH: Humility.
Classification: LCC BJ1533.H93 B45 2023 (print) | LCC BJ1533.H93 (ebook) |
DDC 179/.9--dc23/eng/20230501
LC record available at https://lccn.loc.gov/2022051977
LC ebook record available at https://lccn.loc.gov/2022051978

∞ This paper meets the requirements of ANSI/NISO Z39.48-1992
(Permanence of Paper).

24 23   9 8 7 6 5 4 3 2 First printing

Printed in the United States of America

Cover design by Trudi Gershenov
Interior design by Paul Hotvedt

Thomas Cole, "The Course of Empire: Desolation," 1836, oil on canvas,
39 1/5 x 63 1/4 in., Highlights from the Painting Collection, 1858.5,
New-York Historical Society. Digital image created by Oppenheimer Editions.

To my friends who in many stages of my life and career
accompanied me, held me, and challenged me:
I am grateful for your support and love—
and humbled by your gift of true friendship.

CONTENTS

ACKNOWLEDGMENTS

Saying thank you is always a pleasure and a humbling experience, doubly so when humility is your topic. I'm grateful to those who listened to my developing thoughts and offered their own during public events, campus talks, and informal conversations in New Zealand thanks to the Fulbright Specialist program, in Rome, in Bologna at Fondazione per le Scienze Religiose, and in Scotland during visits with colleagues at the universities of St Andrews and Edinburgh. I also exchanged ideas at the International Medieval Congresses in Leeds and Kalamazoo, Michigan, and during meetings of the American Catholic Historical Association, Hispanic Theological Initiative, and College Theology Society.

This project could not have been completed without the key support of the National Endowment for the Humanities Public Scholars grant, which was generously endorsed by Rita George-Tvrtković and Cary J. Nederman. Any views, findings, conclusions, or recommendations expressed in this book do not necessarily reflect those of the National Endowment for the Humanities. Kean University supported this study with a pair of release-time-for-research grants at its inception and a sabbatical at its end. Much of the writing took place in my time as a visiting scholar at Princeton Theological Seminary, to whose librarians I am indebted.

A number of friends and scholars listened to me, read parts of the manuscript, offered research leads, and imparted advice. I am grateful to Tamara Albertini, Peter Antoci, Frank Argote-Freyre, Gerald Blaszczak SJ, Thomas Burnam, David Gibson, Sue Ellen Gronewold, William Hyland, Joseph Kelley,

Xurong Kong, Daniel Marcel La Corte, C. Bríd Nicholson, Omid Safi, Gabriel Said Reynolds, John Sommerfeldt, and Brooks Susman. My colleagues at Kean likely wondered if this book would ever appear as delays intervened. Their advice was sound, but all errors of fact and interpretation are mine.

At Georgetown University Press, I am especially grateful to director Al Bertrand for understanding what I was trying to accomplish and for his skillful and graceful editing. Thanks to the sales, marketing, and publicity teams plus the production and design craftspeople for getting these words out. I am particularly grateful to copyeditor Sarah C. Smith of Arbuckle Editorial and Georgetown's Elizabeth Sheridan.

Our daughter, Grace, is our well-named gift. Now learning to write herself, she accompanied me when I struggled, made me smile, and reminded me to hang on to a thick yellow crayon she gave me years ago, when she was four. I was having a tough time then with a prior book project. She put the crayon on my desk, where it still sits, and said, "Here, Daddy, this will help you write your book." Thank you for being my daughter.

Finally, and as always, I thank Karen, my wife and my best friend, for being her and for helping me be me.

PROLOGUE

The Problem and the Potential

Too humble is half proud.
   Yiddish proverb

Socrates was a humble man. He knew he didn't know much.
Because of this he had an annoying habit of pointing out that
other people didn't know as much as they thought, either. Socrates wanted others to be as humbled by their own ignorance
as he was, but not because he wanted to show them up. He just
realized that the only way to grow was through an honest look
at yourself. Humility helped him do that.

Humility is the first step in self-reflection. It makes us have
second thoughts. It opens us to our ignorance, to our flaws, to
our weaknesses. The next step is trying to fix them. None of
that happens without embracing the lost virtue of humility.
We might call this "learned ignorance."

Let's look at how Socrates figured this out in ancient Athens about 2,500 years ago. Plato, his prize student, recounts the
story in his *Apology*. Socrates's friend Chaerephon visited the
famous oracle at Delphi's temple to Apollo to ask the god if
anyone was wiser than Socrates. Speaking through his mysterious oracle, Apollo said no, Socrates was the wisest man in the
world—which freaked Socrates out. "I said to myself, 'What
is the god saying, and what is his hidden meaning? I am only
too conscious that I have no claim to wisdom, great or small;
so what can he mean by asserting that I am the wisest man in
the world? He cannot be telling a lie; that would not be right
for him.'"

Being Socrates, he started to ask questions. Politicians talk

1

a lot, so Socrates asked them what they thought about things, only to discover that they were fooling themselves and their followers. They couldn't back up what they were talking about. He moved on to the poets and then the artisans, where he found out that they weren't as expert as they said they were, either. While these good Athenians were skilled in their plays and crafts, they weren't also accomplished, insightful, or even well-informed when it came to other topics. They weren't the know-it-alls they tried to act like they were. Even a man renowned for his wisdom came up empty under Socrates's questions. "I reflected as I walked away," Socrates declared, "well, I am certainly wiser than this man. It is only too likely that neither of us has any knowledge to boast of; but he thinks that he knows something which he does not know, whereas I am quite conscious of my ignorance. At any rate it seems that I am wiser than he is to this small extent, that I do not think that I know what I do not know."[1]

It's not that Socrates felt humiliated by his ignorance or that he tried to humiliate his fellow Athenians. In fact, Socrates doesn't name the people he questioned and goes out of his way to protect the identity of that Athenian with a wise reputation. Socrates was being humble—which too many people then and now have overlooked and misunderstood.

Humility is not humiliation. Humility is a virtue, not a vice. Isaac the Syrian, a wise seventh-century person, described humility as itself humble: "What salt is to food, humility is to the virtues, but without humility all our works are in vain."[2] Humility, like salt, brings out the best in others. Without humility, there are no other virtues, and so the medieval Italian poet Dante labeled humility the first virtue. In his *Purgatorio*, the opening book of his three-part *Divine Comedy* describing a journey to the afterlife, Dante describes landing on the terrace called Pride. There he meets the soul of an artist named Oderisi da Gubbio, who had been renowned for illuminating manuscripts. Like others stuck there, Oderisi is still weighed down by the arrogance he carried around during his lifetime. Oderisi strains under a big boulder on his back that bends him double as a reminder of how his earthly pride crushed his spirit.

Oderisi tells Dante he's learned that worldly fame flies away as quickly as a breath. Stuck in purgatory, he sees how his drive for excellence, reputation, and recognition as the best in his field had made him arrogant and disdainful of another artist, Franco of Bologna. Oderisi now admits that he really knew all along that Franco was the better craftsman. Oderisi's pride had blinded his humility on earth; now he is paying the price by toiling through penitence in heaven's waiting room. Dante takes from Oderisi the lesson that he must descend in humility to the Inferno in order to ascend to Paradise. His pilgrimage starts with a truthful recognition of his place in the world. He sees his need for guidance to improve and move along. This doesn't mean that Dante thought less of himself but that, like Socrates, he didn't think more of himself either.[3]

The purpose of this book is to offer a discussion of humility as the lost virtue so we can appreciate and recover humility as Socrates and Dante did. There's more to it than a narrative of humility's decline and fall over the centuries, though we will largely proceed chronologically. This book is an attempt to reclaim a nourishing sense of this virtue for our divided societies. We first encounter classical Greco-Roman mythology, history, and values, then take a close look at ancient Jewish, Christian, and Muslim sources. We'll learn much from these traditions, especially in the Middle Ages, which was the golden age of appreciating humility as a virtue. Enlightenment and contemporary discussions on education in virtue bring us to what humility means—or can and should mean—for community and citizenship today. Wherever possible, I let people from the past speak for themselves by quoting their most illustrative insights directly. We'll see that even people who appreciated humility were not always models of being humble, which is a helpful lesson that the lost virtue, once found or rediscovered, must be practiced or it will go missing again.

What we'll discover is that while humility is in short supply today, there's plenty of me-ism, which is like an infection that makes us sick. Exploring the history of humility can be our path back to courtesy, respect, and good manners in face-to-face exchanges and on social media (which is not always so social), with its protective yet poisonous mask of anonymity. Humility might serve as an alternative to the disease of narcissism that's infected us. We live in a world not of "I'm right and you're wrong" but of "I'm right and you're bad." At its worst, this attitude can deny another person or group's right to an opinion or a place at the table. This is the self-absorbed and divisive product of reckless partisanship, not a well-informed sense of shared citizenship.

Me-ism is also a very bad management principle. If an organization, a school, or a local zoning board is dominated by someone at the top whose idea of leadership is shooting out commands like Zeus's thunderbolts, why would anyone creative or imaginative join? If the leader believes in a pure hierarchy where information and policies only flow down, then there is no chance that the leader can get valuable feedback for course corrections and improvements. The organization can never adapt and improve when top management is aloof and deliberately cuts itself off because it's sure the minions below have nothing helpful and substantial to contribute. Management me-ism is the very opposite of a humility; its self-absorption by definition cuts off the possibility of community, cooperation, and improvement. It has already decided that front-line workers, end-users, and middle managers have nothing to say: we're right, you're not. The rigid dualism of me-ism creates arrogant management that shuts the door to potential.

On the broader scale of civil society and politics, rigid dualism does precisely nothing to move us forward through dialogue, compromise, and consensus. Admittedly, humility may not seem as enticing and exciting since that way of proceeding thrives in the gray middle ground. Yet slogging through the gray has proven time and again to be far less divisive and far more successful than a cartoonish black-and-white opposition. Extremism may make us feel vindicated, but it doesn't move us forward together. Performative political stunts fool us into thinking we're having an impact, but they don't solve problems. Inflexibly wanting to be seen as right all the time can make you wrong if all you do is complain without finding answers to problems by collaborating with others. "No" people tend to be arrogant. "Yes" people tend to be humble— and to get things done. The frightening alternative to a life informed by humility has been the death of civility and practical results. Some people prefer to be right and dead in the water than wrong and rowing together toward a better shore.

How to Proceed

This book starts with two strands of thinking about humility in the ancient world that set the table for future explorations of the idea. One strand comes mostly from Greco-Roman culture. It's here that humility gets its bad name, grounded as it is in raw denigration. Disadvantaged ancient people lived on the lower rungs of society, and most wealthy and powerful ancients believed the poor—and certainly the enslaved—should be humbled to the more fortunate, the wealthy, and the well born. Mortals were crushed by gods because they were smaller than divinities. It's a conception of humility not as virtue but as the act of being humiliated by others. That's the root of the me-ism we've experienced working under lousy supervisors and with career climbers, whose rise is fueled by tearing others down. "Me first" means "you second."

The second strand, an important exception to this typical Greco-Roman sense of humility as humiliation, comes from some influential ancient philosophers and religious princi- ples. For them, true learning and self-knowledge begin with the humble recognition that people must start with what they don't understand. This sense develops into the medieval no- tion of learned ignorance, which will be an important part of this book. Such a stance developed over time into a positive sense of the common good: humility as healthy self-effacement in the service of others. Everyone has something to contribute if we can just stop talking and start listening.

We should be aware that those without religious faith can benefit from this material too. You don't have to believe in gods or a God to be humble. A religious believer and a secular humanist can both appreciate and practice humility; they can draw on each other's traditions. Secular humanist and religious traditions can speak starkly and honestly to the human condi- tion. Religious culture can inform your thinking whether you subscribe to a particular faith or not. You can read Bible stories the same way you read Aesop's fables or watch *Sesame Street*: you don't have to believe in talking animals or rambunctious Muppets to get the point.[4]

Early on in this examination of the religious tradition, we encounter the erroneous translation of humility as fear—or, rather, the misconception that the patriarch Abraham's sense of fear of the Lord is the same as fear of flying in a plane or flunking an exam. The ancient Hebrew concept of fear really implies a positive sense of one's smallness versus the grandeur of a divinity's bigness. This sense also includes awe and appre- ciation for a power higher than your own or circumstances be- yond your control. That's not a measure of a person's flaws but rather an accurate and sane self-understanding of our place in a larger universe. Note that self-understanding is quite differ- ent from self-deprecation. When Jesus declares "Blessed are the meek," he means not wimps but rather those of modest status and circumstances. There is a dignity to humility. In Islam, humility is frequently expressed positively as meekness within the contexts of submission and patience, as we'll see. Nowhere does the Bible say, "Blessed are the smug."

Humility, to be productive, must be grounded in dialogue instead of trapped in a self-affirming monologue with ourselves or with those who are already thinking like us. Bias confirmation is subversive and ignites the corrosion of grievance. In her unsettling and demanding book *Caste: The Origins of Our Discontents*, Isabel Wilkerson describes how those in a superior social position can stymie groups they fear will topple their status. She warns us that "a caste system makes a captive of everyone within it." Wilkerson cautions against the notion that being lower on the social scale means being lesser as human beings—which is humiliation, not humility. Arrogance is a problem, too, as Wilkerson also points out in a strong indictment:

> Just as the assumptions of inferiority weigh on those assigned to the bottom of the caste system, the assumptions of superiority can burden those at the top with unsustainable expectations of needing to be several rungs above, in charge at all times, at the center of things, to police those who might cut ahead of them, to resent the idea of undeserving lower castes jumping the line and getting in front of those born to lead.[5]

Humility works against bullying others into accepting our points of view. Humility can fight against willfulness because it begins with the chance that we might be wrong. That realization can be applied to each of us as individuals or to an identity we call home, sometimes dangerously or exclusively: a political group or nation, a race or ethnicity or gender identification, a religion or social class, a neighborhood.

It's hard to talk about humility. How can you say, "I'm proud to be humble" or "Fall in line behind my shining example of humility"? Studying humility is worth the risk of looking in the mirror, specifically to fight against the vice of what ancient Greeks called *hubris*: excessive, presumptuous, self-delusional arrogance that inevitably leads to downfall. Shakespeare's prototypical tragic flaw—a vice—is often the flip side of a virtue: Mr. and Lady Macbeth's ambition becomes lust for ultimate power. This is true of other virtue-vice combinations. Persistence is good, stubbornness isn't. When does commitment to an effort—as small as a fight between brothers or as big as a war—become a dug-in determination to stick to it even when it becomes a losing effort? What is the cost of needing to be right when you're clearly wrong? The lack of humility—a lack that finds its self-generated power in the idea that I have a monopoly on truth and what's good for everyone else—leads to self-righteousness, a deceptive sense of certitude, and at worst the denial of basic human rights, respect, and dignity to anyone a person identifies as the enemy.

Humble people build communities. They share questions and answers. They know they need help. Proud people have to dominate, hoarding power and the spotlight all to themselves. How could anyone below me and who doesn't look or think or pray or vote like me have anything valuable to teach me? Why ask for help, advice, or wise counsel when I have nothing left to learn? We fool ourselves into thinking we can fix everything or, maybe worse, that if my life isn't broken, then nobody else's life is broken, either. An empathy gap can be fatal for civil society. How can you have empathy without humility?

Psychologists tell us that being humble is good for our well-being too. Psychologists, philosophers, and social scientists report a recent increase in research on humility in theory and practice. Those studies demonstrate that humility moderates our ego, tones down blinding self-assurance, and opens us to exploration and conversation. Having an open-eyed view of our strengths and weaknesses is clearly a helpful attitude on which to build self-improvement. That viewpoint also seems to increase our predisposition to serve others. Intellectual humility urges us to rethink our opinions in light of other people's perspectives, more information, and new technology. This is how historians revise interpretations and detectives solve cold cases. Cultural humility allows us to understand how our views are informed but also how they are limited by our personal experiences and group identities. Imperialism looks very different to the people who are colonized. A humble stance leads more frequently to collaboration than competition. Humility promotes teamwork through openness, mutual trust and respect, and mustering cumulative talents from a group of people.[6]

There is, as psychologist David G. Myers writes, the possibility that humility before nature lies at the very heart of science. Humility therefore can have important implications for technology and medicine as well as for legal and social policies. We recognize what we know and don't know, what we can and cannot control, then act accordingly. With new information, we recalibrate. Myers also points out the dangers of arrogance and vanity, such as the impossible idea that we are better than others in most everything. There's also the unrealistic optimism that misfortune will hit others but not us and the self-assuring notion that we are consistently right and others are wrong. Facts matter, and it is arrogant to think you can change them. To make his point, Myers unexpectedly turns to Agatha Christie's Miss Marple as she followed the clues that helped her solve crimes: "It wasn't what I expected. But facts are facts, and if one is proved to be wrong, one must just be humble about it and start again."[7]

Perhaps this is what Pope Francis meant when, speaking from Rome in June 2021, he referred to the worldwide COVID-19 pandemic as "a lesson in humility, showing us that it is not possible to live healthy lives in an unhealthy world, or to go on as we were, without recognizing what went wrong." Anyone who has experienced a car crash, a cancer diagnosis out of nowhere, or a recently discovered congenital defect can testify to that humbling feeling of being out of control. What can we learn from the pandemic's lesson of humility? Francis continued, "Even now, the great desire to return to normality can mask the senseless notion that we can go back to relying on false securities, habits, and projects that aim exclusively at pursuing wealth and personal interests, while failing to respond to global injustice, the cry of the poor, and the precarious health of our planet."[8] That message is a humbling lesson of powerlessness, selfishness, and self-delusion we dare not squander.

Notes

1. Plato, *Last Days of Socrates*, Apology 21a–23c.
2. Louf, *Way of Humility*, 9 (Discourse 57).
3. Dante, *Divine Comedy*, "Purgatorio," canto 11.
4. Wielenberg, "Secular Humility," 41–63; and, more expansively, Wielenberg, *Value and Virtue*.
5. Wilkerson, *Caste*, 182–83.
6. Van Tongeren et al., "Humility," 463–68. A comprehensive look at current research is found in Alfano et al., *Routledge Handbook of Philosophy*; on the psychology of humility in particular, see 373–423. For an analytical state of the field, see Worthington et al., *Handbook of Humility*, particularly concerning the application of the empirical science of humility to interpersonal relationships, businesses, social settings, and political communities.
7. Myers, "Psychology of Humility," 153–75.
8. Pope Francis, "Address of His Holiness Pope Francis to the Delegation of the Ecumenical Patriarchate of Constantinople," The Holy See, https://www.vatican.va/content/francesco/en/speeches/2021/june/documents/20210628-patriarcato-costantinopoli.html.

1

ANCIENT NOTIONS
OF HUMILITY

And it is perfectly fair for a man who has a high opinion of
himself not to be put on a level with everyone else.
   Alcibiades, 415 BCE

Alcibiades is a poster child of Greek arrogance—the very
opposite of a virtuous humility. He embodied that terrible
combination of being ambitious and amoral. He was sure
that he was always the smartest person in the room. Living
in Greece in the fifth century BCE at a time when his fellow
Athenians were fighting a death match against their archrivals
the Spartans, Alcibiades repeatedly made decisions based on
what was best for him: what would bring him glory, riches, and
adulation. But then he'd just as quickly backtrack from those
decisions when things went wrong. Alcibiades was clearly a
person who loved praise and hated accountability. Because he
couldn't look himself in the mirror and admit flaws, nothing
was ever his fault. Self-serving and shapeshifting, he turned on
the Athenians to side with the enemy Spartans because he felt
his own people didn't deserve or appreciate him. In the end—
and predictably—Alcibiades's own hubris brought him down.
Before we turn to a fuller account of Alcibiades as a notorious
model of hubris in ancient Greece, we need to trace the root
meanings of the concept of humility.

Humility as Humiliation

Where does the word *humility* come from? Its root is the Latin *humus*, meaning "of the earth"—a coarse, elemental start. Googling dictionary and thesaurus entries on *humble* and *humility* brings up mostly negative descriptions: low self-esteem and submissiveness, docility and timidity, self-abasement, a drooping sense of self-worth, putting yourself down, underestimating your abilities or value, and a lack of self-assurance that pushes against sticking up for yourself. Here we can see how one ancient strand of humility obscured the positive potential of humility as a virtue.

These definitions and connotations could describe not only people who happened to be born at the bottom of ancient society, but also those from higher up who had a fall and were brought low. Their businesses may have failed, they might have gambled and lost politically or socially, or they might have been taken as prisoners of war, a status that crippled not only male soldiers but the women and children in their families back home. These concepts give us the negative idea of a humble person as downtrodden, defeated, crushed, beaten, thrown aside, pressed to nothingness. Some ancient people may have been born lowly, but others had lowliness thrust upon them.

In the Romans' Latin, someone described as *humilis* is "on the ground." This might be a free person of a low status or a slave or foreigner living outside the mighty protection of Roman citizenship. We read of categories of essentially first- and second-class citizens even among free women and men: the *humiliores* are identified as distinct from the wealthy elites or "better people," called *honestiores*. In practical status terms, the *humiliores* were demeaned as the little people and were expected to interact with their betters accordingly: heads down and working manual jobs. Even Romans with a skilled trade, say seamstresses or bakers, were considered ignoble because they worked with their hands, which was akin to the debased work of enslaved people even if the artisans were free citizens.[1]

Greek Mythology

In Greek mythology, we hear more about the excessive, blinding, egocentric, and overblown sense of self that the Greeks called hubris than about humility. The story of Narcissus, which gives us the word *narcissism*, is a good example. Narcissus is a gorgeous, talented, and completely self-absorbed young man. He breaks hearts and believes every compliment thrown his way. One day, he sees his own reflection in a pool of water and is captivated by the good-looking man staring back at him. In some versions of the fable he actually falls for himself by tumbling into the water and drowning. In others, he stabs himself or starves to death in despair because when he reaches into the water to grab his beloved, the image ripples away. Narcissus is certainly the greatest example of overblown self-regard—a legend in his own mind. He has to be at the center of everything. When nobody else is around, Narcissus is a man alone with his best friend.

Another example at least has an explicit warning: the story of Icarus and his father, Daedalus. The father is a craftsman who fashions a set of wings from bird feathers and wax to escape from captivity under King Minos on the island of Crete. Daedalus has made a labyrinth there for the mythological minotaur, who was half man and half bull, but Minos wouldn't let him go. Daedalus was able to escape from his own labyrinth, strap the wings onto himself and his son Icarus, and push off into the sky. Before takeoff, Daedalus warned his son to avoid flying too high, but Icarus was so captivated by his flight that he did just that. As he flapped ever upward with his precarious wings, the sun's heat melted the wax, which pulled the feathers apart and sent Icarus tumbling into the sea to his death. Forgetting good advice, Icarus had overreached and paid the price.

It's the prototypical cautionary tale of going too far too fast without thinking ahead. Icarus's thoughtless recklessness is his own undoing. The Greeks had gods named for these human failings. There is Nemesis, who controls retribution, vengeance, and payback because of hubris. We have the goddess Ate, who nudges women and men to step beyond their bounds and better judgment. She's the goddess of rash, impulsive actions and mischief, something like the Norse (and Marvel) trickster Loki. Ate had not fallen far from the tree of her mother, Eris, the goddess of discord. Eris threw a golden apple into a wedding feast inscribed "To the Fairest." She hadn't been invited to the wedding celebration, so, like a busybody relative nobody liked, she decided to take her chaotic revenge. Zeus wanted no part in making the choice of who got the apple. His wife Hera, his daughter Athena, and the goddess of love Aphrodite all wanted a bite. Zeus assigned Paris, prince of Troy, to the task. Paris gave the apple to Aphrodite, who had promised him the most beautiful woman in the world. That was Helen, married to King Menelaus of Sparta. When Paris kidnapped Helen and took her to Troy, the Greek kings united to bring her back. Homer's *Iliad* and *Odyssey* relate the rest of the tragic story that unraveled as the Trojan War.

Lessons from Thucydides

Self-destructive actions make plain that hubris is at work. These mythological gods and mortals think they can do no wrong. There is no check on their actions; they are blind to the consequences. Like Paris, they see only their own appetites and desires as important—others be damned. Their egos must be fed. But though these are mythological tales devised to teach a point, Greek history also offers examples of real-life hubris in action. Revealing episodes of ancient arrogance in place of humility come from Thucydides, a fifth-century BCE *strategos*, or general, from Athens. He wrote a history of the war between the superpower city-states of Sparta and Athens. Thucydides, with his sharp eye for human folly coupled with military and diplomatic experience, wrote history that repeatedly examines the limits of human foreknowledge and the destruction that comes with not acknowledging those limits.[2]

The Athenians and Spartans, along with their dueling leagues of allies, fought for almost thirty years, with momentum shifting a number of times. But in the end Thucydides makes it clear that the Athenians' final defeat in 404 BCE can be laid at their own feet. In Thucydides's opinion, they overreached for power and prestige. They repeatedly acted with arrogance, even insolence, which clouded their good judgment. Unlike the fate-fueled authors of Greek mythology, Thucydides puts the destiny of human beings in their own hands. He instructs his fellow Greeks not to indict the capricious gods for their ill fortune or to look for prophecies or omens to lead their way. "What made war inevitable," Thucydides writes in the beginning of his account, "was the growth of Athenian power and the fear which this caused in Sparta."

During the Greco-Persian Wars, in which Athens led the defense of Greece, some of the Greek city-states established the Delian League. At first a loose alliance, it became the treasury of an Athenian empire once the Persians had been defeated, with allies paying tribute in cash instead of supplying war matériel. A later Greek historian, Diodorus Siculus, observed bluntly, "For, speaking generally, the Athenians, now that they were making great advances in power, no longer treated their allies fairly, as they had formerly done, but were ruling them harshly and arrogantly."[3]

The Athenians unilaterally moved the treasury from the island of Delos to Athens and then used it as an ancient ATM, spending their allies' money to turn Athens into an architectural showpiece. Critics grumbled that Pericles had built up the Parthenon and other structures on the Acropolis so much that it was decked out like a harlot. The Athenians also forced all the other city-states to use its currency exclusively, which tilted trade and markets in their favor. They tried to legally protect Athenians by attempting to make other courts send Athenian citizens charged with a crime outside Athens back home for trial.

The call of arrogance is heard in a funeral oration that Thucydides attributes to Pericles, the Athenian leader. Delivered in 431 BCE to rally his polis after some losses, Pericles appeals to the great ideals of Athens as "an education for Greece." He declares boldly: "Let me say that our system of government does not copy the institutions of our neighbors. It is more the case of our being a model to others, than of our imitating anyone else." But the very next year, Athens was struck down physically (and, to read Thucydides, emotionally) by a plague that ripped through the city-state.

Athens's strut now stumbled. "The most terrible thing of all," Thucydides reports, "was the despair into which people fell when they realized that they had caught the plague; for they would immediately adopt an attitude of utter hopelessness, and, by giving in in this way, would lose their powers of restraint." Abandoning the law and order that Pericles had exalted as Athens's gift to the rest of the Greeks, the inhabitants of Athens broke out into fits of pleasure-seeking, avarice, and lawlessness. The people turned on Pericles, saying that his war policies had called down the wrath of the gods in the form of disease and military defeat. In the end was the one thing that Pericles admits they did not see coming: the plague that took many lives, Pericles's included. Even the greatest city-state was not, it turned out, immune to an epidemic that Athens couldn't control by its will or personality.

As the Peloponnesian War dragged on, we repeatedly see the Athenians' notion that they were invincible lead them to make dumb decisions. Pericles, for all his arrogance, saw it coming. He had cautioned early on that the Athenians could beat themselves only if they made the mistakes of trying to expand the empire during the war and of starting trouble where it didn't exist. "What I fear," Pericles warned in what sounds in hindsight like a prophecy, "is not the enemy's strategy, but our own mistakes." That's exactly what happened. As the war stalled in Greek territory, the Athenians got the bright idea that if they took the fight elsewhere, they could beat the Spartans and their allies by making them divert soldiers and resources. Athens set its sights on Sicily, completely underestimating the size of the place and the firm resistance of its inhabitants.

Lured by reports of Sicilian silver loads and lavish temples and treasuries, the Athenians gathered to discuss an expedition. Here we again meet Alcibiades when the young and craven politician debated against the experienced, cautious general Nicias. It was the wrong time for such an ambitious effort, Nicias argued. If they went, they would have adversaries at their back in Greece and would make new ones in Sicily. Athens would be divided and vulnerable: "This is no time for running risks or for grasping at a new empire before we have secured the one we have already." His argument in the debate was that Sicily was no danger; if there was trouble they'd be far from help; and even if they won, the colony would be hard to rule from such a great distance.

Alcibiades wanted to lead the expedition to Sicily because he thought that if he commanded a great victory, he'd rise in stature and fill his bank account to support his luxurious hobbies, like horse breeding. He gave a classic "it's all about me" speech, recounting his Olympic victories in chariot racing and

what he'd done for Athens. He sounds like the typical dema-
gogue, saying that everything he did was for the people and
the state: As I rise, so do you. Only I can fix it.

> Again, though it is quite natural for my fellow citizens to
> envy me for the magnificence with which I have done things
> in Athens, such as providing choruses and so on, yet to the
> outside world this also is evidence of our strength. Indeed,
> this is a very useful kind of folly, when a man spends his own
> money not only to benefit himself but his city as well. And it
> is perfectly fair for a man who has a high opinion of himself
> not to be put on a level with everyone else. . . . What I know
> is that people like this—all, in fact, whose brilliance in any
> direction has made them prominent—are unpopular in their
> lifetimes.

Delirious with war fever, the Athenians planned a huge
force, but the expedition proceeded poorly, and the Athenians
blamed Alcibiades. Meanwhile, he was accused of desecrating
statues of the messenger god Hermes around the city and was
also suspected of hedging his fortunes by conspiring with the
Spartans (of all people) to overthrow Athenian democracy. He
looked guilty when, after agreeing to sail back to Athens from
Sicily to stand trial, he ran away and ended up on the Spartan
side. Always slippery, he gave a convoluted speech to the Spartans in which he tried to both praise and criticize democracy,
then offered to help the Spartans and the Sicilians against the
Athenians. When the Spartans, like his native Athenians, tired
of his games, Alcibiades tried to cuddle up to the Greeks' old
enemy the Persians. Bizarrely, he was briefly able to restore
his reputation with the fickle Athenians and was given command of some ships against the Spartan force. But Alcibiades
couldn't help himself. He again alienated the Athenians and
ended up in Asia Minor under a Persian governor, who had

him killed when pressed by the angry Spartans. Alcibiades justifiably ended up being hated by all and trapped by his own triple-dealing shenanigans. He had worn out his welcome everywhere. He had only his hubris to blame. Narcissist to the end, he probably didn't.

Athens was Alcibiades writ large. Just as Alcibiades's arrogance brought him down, so too did the Athenians' arrogance finally lead to their own defeat. No longer able to beat back the Spartans and their increasingly large set of allies, the Athenians agreed to pitiless peace terms in 404 BCE. The long walls that had fortified Athens were pulled down. The great Athenian fleet was reduced to just twelve triremes. Ancient Greeks such as Thucydides and Nicias had seen this coming: they had a strong sense that Athenian arrogance would bring the city down.

These Greeks did not, however, offer a corresponding positive definition of humility. Consider Polemaios around 120 BCE. An inscription about him appears at a Greek sanctuary called Klaros in today's Turkey. It extols his good deeds and achievements without a hint of modesty:

> He was crowned with prizes at sacred games, bringing the renown of these to his fatherland, and he offered the appropriate sacrifices to the gods. In his eagerness from the beginning to enable everyone alike to join in the conduct of his life, he distributed sweetmeats, allowing them to share in the abundance of his livelihood. Because he considered as splendid not only the renown imparted to his life and his fatherland by the achievements of his body, but also the renown from taking charge of public affairs with statesmanlike speech and actions, he went away to the city of Rhodes, and there he attended the best teachers; his conduct during his residence there was blameless and trouble-free, and worthy of each of the cities. After this, when he was appointed as theoros

to the city of Smyrna, he offered the customary sacrifices
to the gods, along with the man who was chosen with him,
in a manner worthy of each of the peoples, and he gave the
money that was allocated to him for the sacrifice back to the
people. He stayed on afterwards, and there also he attended
the best teachers. He received a fitting commendation of his
whole residence there.[4]

In the Greco-Roman world, if you did it, it ain't braggin'.

Ancient Countercurrents

But hubris and elite reputation management aren't the full
story of ancient ideas about humility. Another strand was influential for the development of humility as well as instructive
for us today.

Aristotle (384–322 BCE) offers us an important alternative
approach. Like his philosophical grandfather Socrates, who
saw humility as his starting point for learning, Aristotle presented this virtue as an exercise in self-reflection and therefore
self-improvement. Aristotle used the word *excellence* (Greek,
arete) to describe what we call a virtue. For Aristotle, a virtue
sat in the middle point between two vices—a mean between
two extremes. Bravery, for example, offsets cowardice on one
side, with foolhardiness or recklessness on the other.

Pride is not necessarily a negative attribute for Aristotle. In
its positive sense, pride sits between arrogance or hubris and
a belittling sense of being unworthy (selling yourself short).
We can take this middle ground of good pride as humility in
the sense we've been pursuing. Elsewhere, Aristotle describes
a person who is self-humiliating as acting in a defeatist manner
and not showing earned self-confidence, which is praiseworthy. Short-changing yourself is not proper pride or humility;
it's tearing yourself down improperly, degrading yourself and

letting others dump on you. But Aristotle clarifies that even such people on this wrong side of the equation are not bad (since they haven't done anything evil). They're simply mistaken or misguided.

Think of hubris and arrogance in terms of a vain person. You swagger though you don't deserve it: you haven't earned praise. Even if you have merit, maybe you're not as great as you think you are, so your feelings of self-worth could be excessive. Pride understood as a virtue means that you are appropriately proud of something that you accomplished. Aristotle cautions us that people full of hubris are unduly proud and puffed up. Not only that, but they often shame others, even cruelly, as if they like putting others down in order to raise themselves up. Some are so vulgar in their bullying arrogance that they even seem to like—or to need—to demean other human beings. In our workplaces, we know the climbers who kiss up and punch down. Their path to feeling better about themselves entails degrading and hurting their coworkers. That approach is certainly not virtuous; in fact, that kind of behavior can lead to painful payback.

Finding balanced humility is the result of habit. Aristotle indicated that practice is how character is cultivated. We are what we repeatedly do, which is encouraging because it means we can cultivate proper pride, moderation, and humility as excellences or virtues. To know the good, to use the proverb, is to do the good. Plato and his student Aristotle took it a step further: doing good makes you good. It's like weightlifting: the more you lift, the more you can lift. That's why they were interested in education. Practice develops skills, habits, and, in this case, character. Aristotle gives us two examples, one mundane and one lofty. By practicing the lyre and performing just acts, we become accomplished lyre players and just people. Of course, bad habits can develop as well. The more haughty you act, the more degrading and contemptuous of others you become. If acting virtuously breeds virtue, then certainly it's also true that acting with vice can tear you and others down. Vice is poison. Virtue is nutrition.

We can see all these ideas coming together in a specific passage of Aristotle's *Nicomachean Ethics* where he considers hubris and haughtiness. He warns that people who are highborn, powerful, or wealthy often think they are better than anyone else and deserve praise and honor naturally. In our terms, we might say they were born on third base and think they hit a triple. Or that because they're rich, they think they're smart or a good leader. Aristotle disagrees: being born in fortunate circumstances has nothing to do with a good soul or a savvy mind. He says Greek society gets it wrong: "Yet in truth, only the good human being is honorable, though he who has both goodness and good fortune is deemed even worthier of honor." The key is not fame or honor, money or good luck, but virtue. You can have all of those worldly things and still not have a good soul, a sharp mind, or a virtuous disposition: "But those who possess such goods in the absence of virtue do not justly deem themselves worthy of great things, nor are they correctly spoken of as great-souled: in the absence of complete virtue, neither of these is possible." If you have a lot of stuff but don't have a good soul, you certainly don't have pride or humility in the right sense of an excellent character.

> And people who possess such goods become haughty and hubristic because, in the absence of virtue, it is not easy to deal with the goods of fortune in a suitable manner. Although not in fact being able to deal with these goods and supposing themselves to be superior to others, they look down on them, while they themselves act in whatever random way. For they imitate the great-souled man without being like him, and they do this wherever circumstances per-

mit. They do not perform the deeds that accord with virtue, then, but they look down on others nonetheless.[5]

Like sincerity, you can't fake humility. But when humility is present—either innately or cultivated through habit—it's a virtue that shines not only for the humble person but also bathes those around her.

Notes

1. Wengst, *Humility*, 4–15.
2. The following accounts and quotations are taken largely from Thucydides, *History of the Peloponnesian War*, particularly I.23, 144; II.47–65; and VI.8–16.
3. Diodorus Siculus, *Library of History*, XI.70.3.
4. Supplementum Epigraphicum Graecum 39.1243, http://www.attalus.org/docs/seg/s39_1243.html.
5. To explore Aristotle on issues of hubris, see his *Nicomachean Ethics*, books 2 and 4. For this particular section where he lays out the dangers of haughtiness, see Aristotle, *Aristotle's Nicomachean Ethics*, 177–78 (Book IV, ch. 3, 1124a–b).

2

HUMILITY IN A BIBLICAL KEY

> For all who exalt themselves will be humbled, but all who
> humble themselves will be exalted.
>
> *Jesus, ca. 30 CE (Luke 18:14)*

With these competing Greek notions of humility in mind, we
now explore the biblical contribution to the idea of humility,
bearing in mind that nonreligious people can still benefit from
the wisdom and insights of a biblical culture of stories and
proverbs meant to teach the way to a good life. We should also
note that positive and negative understandings of humility sat
side by side, challenging ancient societies just as much as modern cultures today.

Humility in the Jewish Tradition

We start with a misunderstood notion closely related to humility—fear of the Lord, which is closely connected with the
sense of awe in Hebrew. For the first ancient Israelites, fear
did not mean people feared God as we might fear a root ca-
nal. They were in awe of a power greater than themselves: a
foundational disposition of reverence, obedience, and respect.
You get a sense of Yahweh's approval of this sense of fear in a
representative passage from the prophetic book of Isaiah:

> But this is the one to whom I will look,
> to the humble and contrite in spirit,
> who trembles at my word. (Isaiah 66:2)[1]

Ancient Israelites rationally measured their human smallness relative to Yahweh's divine big-ness. For them, fear of the Lord is the beginning of wisdom, according to Proverbs 9:10, although this biblical book begins with a description that's worded a bit differently. The first passage says the fear of the Lord is the beginning of knowledge. Over a few verses, the author advises that believers should obey God's will in a spirit of reverence, discipline, and obedience in the face of a divine being who's full of love and learning (Proverbs 1:1–9).

The Jewish tradition often refers to this kind of reverential awe or fear in the context of encountering someone who can teach you—in this case Yahweh, but also human elders. Like Socrates's lesson, what's key to our education is that we must realize that we need their tutoring. It takes a humble and self-aware person to say, "I don't know." A good place to explore this view is in the book of Sirach, particularly in its first chapter, where the payoff of this conception of fear is humility.

> The fear of the Lord is glory and exultation,
>   and gladness and a crown of rejoicing.
> The fear of the Lord delights the heart,
>   and gives gladness and joy and long life. . . .
> To fear the Lord is fullness of wisdom;
>   she inebriates mortals with her fruits;
> she fills their whole house with desirable goods,
>   and their storehouses with her produce.
> The fear of the Lord is the crown of wisdom,
>   making peace and perfect health to flourish.
> She rained down knowledge and discerning comprehension,
>   and she heightened the glory of those who held her fast.

After this flood of promises and enticements, the ancient Israelites might have asked: OK, all fine and good, but how do we come to this reward? The answer involves a slow listening and learning, grounded in the understanding that by fearing the greater power of Yahweh—or for a nonbeliever, someone who simply knows more than I do—I will become a more informed, more grounded, and maybe even a downright better and more balanced person.

> Those who are patient stay calm until the right moment,
>   and then cheerfulness comes back to them.
> They hold back their words until the right moment;
>   then the lips of many tell of their good sense.
> In the treasuries of wisdom are wise sayings,
>   but godliness is an abomination to a sinner.

We have here a sequence: fear the Lord, and you will grow in the gift of wisdom. Growing in that gift requires discipline and keeping the commandments on an equal level with others in your community, not setting yourself above them.

> If you desire wisdom, keep the commandments,
>   and the Lord will lavish her upon you.
> For the fear of the Lord is wisdom and discipline,
>   fidelity and humility are his delight.
> Do not disobey the fear of the Lord;
>   do not approach him with a divided mind.
> Do not be a hypocrite before others,
>   and keep watch over your lips.
> Do not exalt yourself, or you may fall
>   and bring dishonor upon yourself.
> The Lord will reveal your secrets
>   and overthrow you before the whole congregation,
> because you did not come in the fear of the Lord,
>   and your heart was full of deceit. (Sirach 1:11–12, 16–19,
>   23–30)[2]

It's not that the readers of Sirach thought that they were worthless as human beings. Instead, they recognized they weren't divine. For this reason, Moses takes off his shoes in front of the mysterious bush that's on fire yet doesn't burn away. But divinity need not be involved. Consider a moment when you realize a speaker is in command of material you don't understand, or an electrician is rewiring a lamp you can't. In the presence of a master, you watch and learn. It's something like that: Moses knows he's in the presence of something consequential that he doesn't understand but needs to respect. He comes to a realistic sense of where he stands in the context of a grand universe bigger than the soil and water around him. Some helpful Hebrew words related to this sense of self are transliterated as *zenua* (to be humble) and *anav* (to be meek); in both cases they should be taken positively in the vein of what we've learned about self-awareness from Socrates and Aristotle.

Self-understanding is not self-deprecation. It means we know what we don't know. We also know we're no more or less inherently valuable than others around us. It's from this humble moment, Sirach teaches, that you can bow to education and rise to virtue, which was a habit Plato and Aristotle recommended that we cultivate.

> If you are willing, my child, you can be disciplined,
>   and if you apply yourself you will become clever.
> If you love to listen you will gain knowledge,
>   and if you pay attention you will become wise.
> Stand in the company of the elders.
>   Who is wise? Attach yourself to such a one.
> Be ready to listen to every godly discourse,
>   and let no wise proverbs escape you.
> If you see an intelligent person, rise early to visit him;
>   let your foot wear out his doorstep. (Sirach 6:32–36)

A key to progress is finding a good mentor and sitting at her feet, humbly acknowledging that we have a lot to learn. There is a sense of being indebted to the teacher and therefore grateful that someone took the time to bring you along. Elsewhere, Sirach focuses more directly on humility. The text makes the point that even after we have achieved a skill or understanding on our own, or because another person stopped to show us the way, we should go about our tasks quietly and competently without creating a big show of it.

> Do not make a display of your wisdom when you do
>   your work,
>   and do not boast when you are in need. . . .
> My child, honor yourself with humility,
>   and give yourself the esteem you deserve.
> Who will acquit those who condemn themselves?
>   And who will honor those who dishonor themselves?
>   (Sirach 10: 26, 28–29)

Notice that Sirach teaches about proper pride, like Aristotle did in finding the balance between hubris and humiliation. If you did well, be proud, but don't make a fuss.

Now we come to the socially threatening irony that ancient Hebrews offered their Greek and Roman neighbors. As Sirach put it:

> The wisdom of the humble lifts their heads high, and seats
>   them among the great. (Sirach 11:1)

Proverbs puts the topsy-turvy idea this way:

> The fear of the Lord is instruction in wisdom,
>   and humility goes before honor. (Proverbs 15:33)

Throughout Hebrew and then Christian scriptures, we find stories and teachings that threaten to undermine the Greco-Roman social system. The poor and those of low social status have inherent dignity and could rise from their beleaguered status. Fear brings learning and honor, glory and greatness. The humbled are exalted while those who exalt themselves will be toppled. The first are last, and the last are first. The servants and enslaved are saved. The meek inherit the earth. The weak are strong, and the strong are weak. The hungry are fed, but the rich are sent away empty. The lowly hear the message and are pumped full of gladness. The haughty and the arrogant, the oppressors and the elites, fall.

These words were nonsense to most Greeks and Romans who missed the point that no matter how high you are in society, your status doesn't make you better. This was the crippling lesson the Athenians had to learn. Everyone needs to heed advice and to realize that however culturally and politically powerful you might be, you are not entirely in charge, and you can easily act immorally. This is why Yahweh frequently has to send prophets like Jeremiah, Ezekiel, and Daniel to warn recalcitrant people to get in shape or else. The prophet Isaiah, for example, puts the arrogant on notice in a passage where he defines sin as the hubris of thinking we know it all:

> The haughty eyes of people shall be brought low,
>   and the pride of everyone shall be humbled;
>   and the Lord alone will be exalted on that day.
> For the Lord of hosts has a day
>   against all that is proud and lofty,
>   against all that is lifted up and high;
> against all the cedars of Lebanon,
>   lofty and lifted up;
>   and against all the oaks of Bashan;

> against all the high mountains,
>   and against all the lofty hills;
>   against every high tower,
> and against every fortified wall;
>   against all the ships of Tarshish,
>   and against all the beautiful craft.
> The haughtiness of people shall be humbled,
>   and the pride of everyone shall be brought low;
>   and the Lord alone will be exalted on that day. (Isaiah
>   2:11–17)

More concisely, the author of Proverbs says:

> Pride goes before destruction,
>   and a haughty spirit before a fall. (Proverbs 16:18)

Let's gather together these Jewish teachings to consider a helpful story of intellectual humility from the first century BCE, when the Hebrew Bible was just about coming into its final form. We read during this historical period that the rabbis praised meekness and humility in scholars, who easily fall into arrogance, notably when their learning gathered prestige and honor. Two competing groups of rabbis discussed a particular legal matter about ritual purity over three years. One group surrounded the leading scholar Hillel and the other a sage named Shammai. Finally, Yahweh's voice came down from heaven with the verdict that Hillel's school was correct. Why? A contemporary commentary explains: "Because they were kindly and modest, they studied their own rulings and those of Beth Shammai, and were even so humble as to mention the actions of Beth Shammai before theirs."[3]

You don't have to be a well-read scholar like Hillel's rabbis to practice humility. There is a lesson on personal humility from Erev Yom Kippur, the annual day of atonement that falls in September or October. Before asking Yahweh to forgive them on Yom Kippur, faithful Jews on the day before (*erev*) humbly ask forgiveness from those they have offended—up to three times if necessary. The very act of admitting sin and acknowledging that you fell short—and then of asking forgiveness directly from the person whom you hurt by your words or actions—is an act of humility and contrition.

Making sincere and tangible atonement is not easy; it might even be easier to face Yahweh in prayer than your sister-in-law on her porch. The medieval Spanish sage Maimonides (1138–1204) in his *Mishneh Torah* commented on the laws of repentance and Yom Kippur. He made the point that earthly sins must be atoned face-to-face, however uncomfortable or awkward that conversation might be: "for sins committed against a fellow man, as when a person either injured or cursed or robbed his neighbor, [are] never pardoned unless he compensates his neighbor and makes an apology. Even though he has made the compensation, the wrongdoer must appease the injured person and ask his pardon. Even if he only annoyed him with words he must apologize and beg for forgiveness." The penitent must approach with humility, but the transgressed must also act graciously and not with condescension: "One must not show himself cruel by not accepting an apology; he should be easily pacified, and provoked with difficulty. When an offender asks his forgiveness, he should forgive wholeheartedly and with a willing spirit. Even if he has caused him much trouble wrongfully, he must not avenge himself, he must not bear a grudge. This is the way of the stock of Israel and their upright hearts."[4]

We learn from this practice of Erev Yom Kippur that restitution can lead to transformation of at least one and maybe both parties, but only if we realize that we need forgiveness and have the courage to ask for, to receive, and to bestow it. Relying on Yahweh's mercy in this religious context or on the graciousness of the offended in any context, we recognize that we are often self-focused instead of other-oriented. Being self-focused does not help us to practice humility, but being other-oriented can. In the Hebrew tradition, humility is a building block of *tikkun olam*: keeping the community together by repairing divisions and pursuing justice.

Humility in the Christian Mind

Ancient Greeks and Romans were confounded by Christian belief, like some of the language in the Hebrew tradition, because it turned their worlds upside down. Christians believe that God became a human being named Jesus. The theological concept of God becoming human upended ancient conversations about humility in a very dramatic and influential way. This divine action in turn ennobled all human beings, even if they were in the basement of society in Jerusalem. Humility valued as a virtue in Hebrew scripture was strange enough; but why would God, a divine being, deliberately fall so far as to get down and dirty as a human?

According to Christian tradition, God not only took on actual human form—called the incarnation, meaning literally "en-fleshed"—but did so in a particularly humble way. His mother Mary was young, poor, and of low status, as well as unmarried. Her fiancé was a man named Joseph, a manual laborer. Jesus apprenticed under his father as an artisan or tradesman, making a meager living by the work of his hands. For Christians, God was living humbly in out-of-the-way Nazareth, an inauspicious start in the ancient world where social standing and political connections meant everything.

Nothing in this scenario would have impressed a Greek or Roman. For the big players in Greco-Roman society, lowliness (in the Greek of the gospel narratives: *tapeinophrosynē*) was all about bottom-dwelling rank, which is how they measured worth. Yet along comes the God-man Jesus who intentionally embraces lowliness and the humble status of parents with no prestige or social standing. The vice is now made a virtue and raises everyone else in that same status to a higher plane. Since the first Christians were Jews, they would have been receptive to the notion that a humble birth was not valueless, given the scriptural conceptions of humility and fear of the Lord as virtues.[5]

For Christians, Jesus is the model of humility by the very action of the incarnation, but there are other humble heroes in Christian scriptures. Jesus's herald, by tradition his cousin John the Baptist, for all of his fame knows that he himself is not the anointed one. We're told that John is an outcast who should be ignored by polite and proper society. John lives in the desert, wears rough clothes, and eats off the land with a diet of honey and locusts. He cries out like a crazy person on a street corner with a sign saying, "The end of the world is Thursday!" Why listen to him? But for Christians, John the Baptist is a humble man preparing the way for a humble God. John's task is to get people ready for Jesus and then get out of the way. He declares that he's not even worthy to untie Jesus's sandals. Once Jesus appears, John knows he must yield. His job is done. As John says, referring to Jesus: "He must increase, but I must decrease" (John 1:27; 3:30). The Romans' client king Herod executes John as a criminal with a wave of his hand. John is decapitated, and his ministry is further disgraced when his head is carried into Herod's throne room on a serving platter like the next course in a banquet feast.

Jesus's Ministry of Humility

A centerpiece of Jesus's ministry, repeated often, is that the humble should rejoice. Jesus said this to both big crowds and also to his bickering disciples who were jostling to be next in prestige after him. Maybe the most striking litany of this theme is in what's called the Sermon on the Mount. Gospel writer Matthew sets the scene: Jesus's reputation for healing and wisdom is spreading fast. The crowds grow. In some other gospel scenes, he has to stand in a boat pulled back from the shore to keep from being crushed. In this scene, Jesus stands atop a mountain so more people can see and hear his lyrical message:

> Blessed are the poor in spirit, for theirs is the kingdom of heaven.
> Blessed are those who mourn, for they will be comforted.
> Blessed are the meek, for they will inherit the earth.
> Blessed are those who hunger and thirst for righteousness, for they will be filled.
> Blessed are the merciful, for they will receive mercy.
> Blessed are the pure in heart, for they will see God.
> Blessed are the peacemakers, for they will be called children of God.
> Blessed are those who are persecuted for righteousness' sake, for theirs is the kingdom of heaven.
> Blessed are you when people revile you and persecute you and utter all kinds of evil against you falsely on my account. Rejoice and be glad, for your reward is great in heaven, for in the same way they persecuted the prophets who were before you. (Matthew 5:3–12)

This list, known as the Beatitudes, is startlingly out of touch with the wider Greco-Roman social and value system in which Jesus and his Jewish followers lived. Jesus was speaking to their values, not the Roman system, by preaching in the Jewish tradition. For the poor, Jesus's idea that the meek and the poor in spirit—the humble—are blessed and not worthless must have been hopeful and attractive indeed.

Jesus was heir to his own Jewish tradition of healing relationships by humbly admitting error. Recall the Erev Yom

Kippur practice of asking those you've hurt for forgiveness before asking Yahweh for pardon on the day of atonement. In the same vein, Jesus counseled that if you are going to court or to offer a gift at an altar, take a detour and try to settle the conflict with your adversary, or reconcile with an estranged sister and brother first. Learn to ask forgiveness: look within and recognize your own failings with open eyes. Stop being a hypocrite. Understand who you are by seeing the plank of wood in your own eye before pointing out the speck of sawdust in somebody else's. That attitude of introspective humility would have made Socrates proud.[6]

Jesus had told a parable about the tax collector and the Pharisee who were praying near the Temple in Jerusalem. The Pharisee, who was well placed and respected in his community, ostentatiously thanked Yahweh that he was not like the unwashed herd of thieving, adulterous rogues. You can almost hear him spit when mentioning those lesser mortals as he stood apart from them. He prayed twice a week and boasted that he gave 10 percent of his income to charity. This showy Pharisee was specifically full of contempt when comparing himself to the tax collector, a Jew nearby who was shunned because tax collectors were known to skim off the top of the taxes they collected for the Romans. Curiously to those who still didn't get what he was saying, Jesus sided with the tax collector who didn't dare make a spectacle of himself because he was so aware of his own faults. The tax collector didn't even get that close to the Temple or look up to heaven when he prayed, "God, be merciful to me, a sinner!" The moral of the story, Jesus told his audience, was that Yahweh favored not the self-righteous Pharisee but the demeaned tax collector. "For all who exalt themselves will be humbled," this mystifying rabbi taught, "but all who humble themselves will be exalted" (Luke 18:9–14).

The notion that God humbly takes on human form specifically to serve others is illustrated in the shocking gospel scene

where Jesus acts like a servant on what Christians commem-
orate as Holy Thursday (John 13:4–15). Taking on the role of
a servant performing a menial task, Jesus rolls up his sleeves,
kneels in a subservient position, washes his disciples' feet, and
dries them with a towel he'd wrapped around his waist. Then,
he commands his dumbfounded disciples to copy what he'd
just done. The master, Jesus, the son of God, had become a
servant to wash their feet. If his followers are to lead, they must
also be servants. As we see in the next chapter, medieval nuns
and monks saw themselves as communities of servants just
like this: each one taking care of the other. Over centuries, a
traditional title of the pope growing from this gospel episode
and monastic examples will be *servus servorum Dei*: the servant
of the servants of God. (Imagine aiming for a tombstone that
reads: "Here lies so-and-so. He washed feet.") In addition, the
next day Jesus was crucified, which was a torturous death reserved for criminals and runaway or rebellious slaves.

Humility in the Early Churches

The idea of God recommending—for Christians, embody-
ing—human humility as a virtue was a key part of the first
attractive messages about Jesus after his earthbound ministry.
We see this in the letter that the apostle Paul sent to the Philippians twenty years after Jesus's ministry around 55 CE. Philippi
was a wealthy city in Greece. It was also the city where in 42
BCE Julius Caesar's heir Octavian (later Augustus) and his ally
Marc Antony caught up with and defeated Brutus and Cassius,
the ringleaders of Caesar's assassination two years before on
the infamous Ides of March. In his letter, Paul brings the point
of Jesus's praiseworthy humility home quite hard:

> Do nothing from selfish ambition or conceit, but in humility
>   regard others as better than yourselves. Let each of you
>   look not to your own interests, but to the interests of

> others. Let the same mind be in you that was in
>   Christ Jesus,
> who, though he was in the form of God,
>   did not regard equality with God
>   as something to be exploited,
> but emptied himself,
>   taking the form of a slave,
>   being born in human likeness.
> And being found in human form,
>   he humbled himself
>   and became obedient to the point of death—
>   even death on a cross.
> Therefore God also highly exalted him
>   and gave him the name
>   that is above every name. (Philippians 2:3–9)

We see here another step in the development of humility as something positive. Paul was a Jew who believed in Jesus as the prophesied messiah, and so he brought the Jewish concept of humility as praiseworthy to his missionary preaching. He was writing to a population of believers and potential converts that was increasingly gentile and who understood humility quite differently. In order to embrace Jesus as divine, gentiles had to abandon their cultural view of humility as humiliation—or else the incarnation was nonsense.

Another example of early Christian views of humility dates from just before the first century CE ended, perhaps 96 or 97. That's when a letter attributed to Clement, who was probably head of the Christian community in Rome, arrived in Corinth. (As the centuries progress, this person will be called the bishop of Rome and, in turn, the Roman Catholic pope.) Clement's letter is the earliest Christian document apart from the Gospels and missionary letters. Corinth was no spiritual paradise: in the ancient world, what happened in Corinth stayed in Corinth. As an isthmus city, it was a crossroads of the Mediterranean that drew people from all over the ancient world. There's evidence of gods and goods from Egypt, Rome, Greece, and Syria, among other places. There were Jewish, Christian, and polytheistic ideas, languages, and concepts jumbled together.

Clement's First Letter is important for humility's history because it represents the development of humility as a positive virtue a half century after Jesus. Just as Moses understood his proper place in relation to Yahweh, these second and third generations of Christians were learning their place in relation to the Other they called Jesus. That insight was the source of their personal growth.

> Let us then, brothers [and sisters], be humble and be rid of all pretensions and arrogance and silliness and anger. Let us act as Scripture bids us, for the Holy Spirit says: "Let not the wise man boast of his wisdom or the strong man of his might or the rich man of his wealth. But let him that boasts, boast of the Lord; and so he will seek Him out and act justly and uprightly."

At the same time, Clement condemns "those arrogant and disorderly fellows," who instigate, deceive, and boast. Hypocrites, particularly among those professing the new faith of Christianity, aren't worthy of the humble God-man Jesus.

> It is to the humble that Christ belongs, not to those who exalt themselves above his flock. The scepter of God's majesty, the Lord Jesus Christ, did not come with the pomp and pride of arrogance, though he could have done so. But he came in humility.

Clement from Rome prays that believers in Corinth will receive humility so they can open themselves to divine will and correction while striving to be more like biblical models and specifically Jesus.

> You see, dear friends, the kind of example we have been given. And so, if the Lord humbled himself in this way, what should we do who through him have come under the yoke of his grace? . . . The humility and obedient submissiveness of so many and so famous heroes have improved not only us but our fathers before us, and all who have received His oracles in fear and sincerity.[7]

This idea of a divine being or just a well-respected human leader praising the last rung on the ladder—indeed, declaring that it is best to deliberately grasp that last rung as your first choice—can be puzzling. But to Jews seeking a savior, be it political or religious, from oppression, this message of the Hebrew scriptures and then of Jesus and his followers was enthralling. For gentiles too the promise that your lowly state would be raised, and that it already contained dignity and value, was very appealing. Humility, used by others to oppress, was now offered as a virtue, a grace, even a blessing. It was this more positive conception of humility as a virtue and not humiliation as a vice that exploded in the Middle Ages.

Notes

1. All biblical passages in this and subsequent chapters are drawn from the New Revised Standard Version.
2. Another title is Ecclesiasticus, which should not be confused with the book of Ecclesiastes. Sirach appears in the Catholic canon sometimes referred to as the Catholic bible but not in Jewish scripture or the Protestant collection of biblical books. Sirach is gathered into what Catholics call the deuterocanonical (or second canon) texts. Protestants and Jews refer to these additional texts as the Apocrypha.

3. *'Erubin*, 13b in I; Epstein, ed. and trans., *The Babylonian Talmud. Seder Mo'ed*, 4 vols. (London: The Soncino Press, 1938), II.85–86. For a fuller discussion of this disposition based in Jewish scripture, see Green, "Jewish Ethics," 54–55.

4. Moses Maimonides, *Mishneh Torah. Laws of Repentance*, 2.1, 9, 10 as found in Goodman, *Yom Kippur Anthology*, 44–45, and see 50 for a representative Yom Kippur prayer seeking divine forgiveness "in deep humility and contrition."

5. Elizabeth A. Johnson gathered the archaeological and other evidence to paint a portrait of Mary, Joseph, and Jesus in their home setting in *Truly Our Sister*, 137–206.

6. Matthew 5:22–25; Luke 12:57–59; Matthew 7:3–5.

7. This passage mirrors Jeremiah 9:23–24, as do I Corinthians 1:31 and II Corinthians 10:17. For this text, see Richardson, *Early Christian Fathers*, 49–53 (sections 13–19) and 69 (section 56).

3

A MEDIEVAL GOLDEN AGE

Humility, queen of the virtues.
Hildegard of Bingen, ca. 1151

Hildegard of Bingen, the "Sybil of the Rhine," was a medieval Renaissance woman: an abbess who established two convents, critic and reformer, botanist and healer, scientist, composer, prophet and preacher, poet and mystic. In her morality play set to music, *Ordo Virtutum* (*Order of the Virtues*), Hildegard presents a dialogue among sixteen virtues, led by their queen, Humilitas, who are squaring off against the devil. They fight over humans trapped on earth who long to rise up to heaven but are enticed by the allures of the world. Their secret weapon? Humility.

Anima is the character representing human beings caught between heaven and hell. Tempted by the devil's promise of fame and fortune, Anima abandons the protection of the virtues to go out into the world and experience her desires. When Anima inevitably returns, worn out like the prodigal son of the parable, Humilitas orders the other virtues to run out to help her. Then they chase the devil away so he can't harm anyone else. They encourage Anima to feel gratitude and to accept their charity. Hildegard's message to her medieval audience is clear. Without the core virtue of humility, none of the other virtues can operate. They don't know what to do without her.[1]

This play isn't the only place where Hildegard presented humility as the queen of the virtues. In another of her works she described her vivid visions, which had started when she was just three years old but later dramatically intensified. She's quite precise about when the blast came and what happened: "When I was forty-two years and seven months old, Heaven was opened and a fiery light of exceeding brilliance came and permeated my whole brain, and inflamed my whole heart and my whole breast, not like a burning but like a warming flame, as the sun warms anything its rays touch." So personally humbled was she by these visions that Hildegard had to be coaxed into trying to translate these flashes of light into words. Hildegard didn't know why she and not others deserved to be blasted by these insights. She was ultimately convinced to dictate them, surely because in one of those visions she heard a voice command, "Cry out therefore, and write thus!" Hildegard talked through her experience of what she called the living light with a nun named Richardis von Stade and a monk called Volmar. They were close friends devoted to helping her spell out what she'd seen and became her collaborators over the course of the ten years it took to record and describe the visions.

Maybe Hildegard's fascination with humility and her attempts to be humble herself were a crack at checking her own pride, stubbornness, impatience, and temper. She was friendly with popes, including Pope Eugenius III, who gave her permission to preach on mission tours—an extraordinary license for a woman at the time. But she was also an outspoken enemy of monks and bishops who opposed her charismatic authority and independence. She got into a long battle with an abbot when she announced that she wanted to leave and set up her own community with like-minded nuns. Hildegard dug in her heels against bishops in Mainz because she had allowed a noble who had been thrown out of the church to be buried in her convent's churchyard when he died. The bishops wanted the body dug up because an excommunicated person could not be buried in sacred soil. Hildegard said the man had repented on his deathbed, but the bishops forcefully pushed back with

an interdict, refusing to let church rituals and liturgies be cel-
ebrated in the convent. After six months during which her actions deprived her own nuns of Mass, chanted prayer, and the
sacraments, the bishops relented. She even stood up to Holy
Roman Emperor Frederick Barbarossa, who was ruling over
her native German territory. Because he supported three suc-
cessive anti-popes favorable to him in opposition to the pope
in Rome, Hildegard called him a madman.

In the descriptions of her visions gathered in *Scivias* (*Know
the Ways*), Hildegard taught that the work of humility is to
crush offenses by rallying the other virtues. This battle versus
vice is exactly how she'd portrayed Humilitas fighting the devil
and the prideful human quest for glory in her play.

> For when a field with great labor is cultivated, it brings forth
> much fruit, and the same is shown in the human race, for
> after humanity's ruin many virtues arose to raise it up again.
> ... Humility always groans, weeps and destroys all offenses,
> for this is its work. So let anyone who wishes to conquer the
> Devil arm himself with humility, since Lucifer fervently flees
> it and hides in its presence like a snake in a hole; for wherever
> it finds him, it quickly snaps him like a fragile thread.

Humility softens hard hearts at the same time that it animates
other virtues so they can repair a broken spirit.

> In this, humility and charity are brighter than the other vir-
> tues, since humility and charity are like a soul and body that
> possess stronger powers than the other powers of soul and
> bodily members. How? Humility is like the soul and charity
> like the body, and they cannot be separated from each other
> but work together, just as soul and body cannot be disjoined
> but work together as long as a person lives in the body. And
> as the various members of the body are subject, according to

their powers, to the soul and to the body, so also the other
virtues cooperate, according to their justice, with humility
and charity. And therefore, O humans, for the glory of God
and for your own salvation, pursue humility and charity;
armed with them, you shall not fear the Devil's snares but
shall have everlasting life.

In another vision, Hildegard sternly condemns people who
choose to be arrogant like Satan rather than acting humbly. In
the traditional story of the cosmic battle between good and
evil, Satan's pride and hubris had gotten the best of him. Not
content with being God's angelic servant, Satan rebelled and
tried to overthrow God, only to find himself thrown out of
heaven forever by the archangels led by the fierce warrior Michael. Hildegard paints a stark picture of his self-destruction:
"Lucifer in heaven devoured himself with hatred and pride."
After that, his first prize was Adam and Eve. Now he prowls
earth trying to entice humans to imitate his pride to bring
other women and men to their own fall. Hildegard describes
Satan and those like him in her own day: "But one who reb-
els and refuses to return to Christ in humility, and continues
in this arrogance, will join the company of those who keep a
stone for a heart and remain in infidelity; and such people refuse to know the glory of the Church's beatitude. For one who
is so obdurate that in his wickedness he will seek no mercy
imitates the ancient serpent."[2]

Hildegard warns that we should positively know our place
and understand our skills. She bluntly asks what good could be
done by stupid, foolish, and careless craftsmen who've puffed
themselves up with an inflated sense of their own skill. If they
build without seeking advice from well-trained artisans with
greater experience, they're asking for trouble from wind and
rain. By contrast, humility, as the queen of the virtues, wears
a glorious golden crown adorned with green and red precious

stones along with white pearls. A mirror hangs on her chest to reflect the goodness of others—in Hildegard's Christian context, naturally starting with Jesus. Humility is central, but it isn't the main event to be worshipped for its own sake. The queen of the virtues is the instrument to praise and inspire others, "for she is the solid foundation of all human good deeds."[3]

Hildegard's medieval play and visions represent the most important period in humility's history, where that second strand of appreciating humility as a virtue dominates over thinking of it in negative terms as the vice of humiliation. Some of the most important early voices of the transition from the ancient to the medieval periods are the trio of Augustine of Hippo in North Africa, Pope Gregory the Great, and Benedict of Nursia, the founder of medieval monasticism. Once we take a close look at their writings, we'll follow their legacy, which Hildegard inherited and expanded. We must take a hard look at how humility was lived out with its benefits and its own temptations too. People writing about humility aren't always humble, and some of their humble practices went too far. Still, what we find in this chapter is that medieval people understood the benefits and balance of humility as a virtue better than others before or since. It was the golden age of humility.

Defining Medieval Humility

When he was asked to name the three most important virtues, a North African theologian named Augustine replied: humility, humility, and humility.[4] How did he come to that ringing statement? The answer: the hard way.

Humility was not a natural attitude for Augustine (354–430), who comes across in his writings as an alpha male who always had to be the center of attention. He lived much of his life in today's Algeria, although he studied and taught in modern Tunisia (ancient Carthage), Rome, and Milan. His biographer said it was hard to be in his circle in any of those diverse places because "Augustine was an imperialist in his friendships."[5]

Once Augustine had gotten his act together in his early thirties, he turned to helping others realize how humility had been a lifesaving virtue. Right after he'd stepped off his career ladder, he and a few friends, along with his mother, Monica, were living in a comfortable country retreat in northern Italy not far from Lake Como. He wrote a short dialogue called *On the Happy Life* from this villa. He described the vice of pride as a huge mountain that stands in the way of contentment, joy, and personal fulfillment. That mountain, he advises from personal experience, "must be very seriously feared and carefully avoided." The mountain is an obstacle that dazzles you with its light and height. Beware its siren song enticing you to climb "the proud pursuit of empty glory." That climb will only cast you down, "for within there is nothing substantial or solid and, with a cracking of the ground-crust beneath, it collapses and swallows up those walking above, puffed up with themselves, and, as they tumble headlong into darkness, it withdraws from them the gleaming dwelling place just barely seen."[6] Having fallen through his own pride, Augustine now warns his readers to avoid this lethal bait-and-switch.

To his credit, in his autobiography entitled *Confessions*, which he wrote around 397–401 CE, Augustine extensively offered himself up as Exhibit A of what a life driven by pride looks like. Augustine indicts his younger self as ambitious, obnoxious, greedy, always acting with uncontrolled emotions and sexual desires, and constantly unsatisfied by answers that settled matters for others but never fully for him.[7] He described himself there as a restless, searching, and arrogant young man who was always on the move and on the make. He recounts burning through a series of philosophical schools and religious communities that intrigued but never fulfilled him.

One scholar concluded that Augustine "exhibited an almost morbid and constantly increasing preoccupation with pride viewed as a major personal problem."[8] He admits he loved being popular, praised, and prized. He knows that he was (and you get the sense that he still is) self-absorbed; if he didn't understand a concept, it was the concept's fault. He was stubborn and willful. Augustine was sure he could prosper on his own merits, yet still, emotionally, he always needed to be surrounded by people telling him how great he was. But Augustine didn't require them to fill him with hot air (though he sounds like he didn't mind); he did that just fine by himself.

Over time, he learned how wrong he was. In one episode he recounts in Confessions, he was reading the Bible as a student of rhetoric and decided that it didn't measure up to the Greco-Roman philosophy and classical literary style he'd been studying and imitating. But looking back from his own middle age of forty-seven, he saw that he had simply been arrogant when he made that presumptuous judgment:

> It was enfolded in mysteries, and I was not the kind of man to enter into it or bow my head to follow where it led. But these were not the feelings I had when I first read the Scriptures. To me they seemed quite unworthy of comparison with the stately prose of Cicero, because I had too much conceit to accept their simplicity and not enough insight to penetrate their depths. It is surely true that as the child grows these books grow with him. But I was too proud to call myself a child. I was inflated with self-esteem, which made me think myself a great man.

Success in rhetoric led Augustine to take up the study of law, where he shamelessly chased ambition and status. "The more unscrupulous I was," he reports in Confessions, "the greater my reputation was likely to be, for men are so blind that they even

take pride in their blindness." At least he's honest enough to
realize now that he was proud of his pride then: "I was pleased
with my superior status and swollen with conceit."

Augustine came to realize that as a student he didn't understand Socrates's fundamental lesson in the humility of learning: inflated with pride and a self-possessed sense of his own
importance, he didn't know what he didn't know. Augustine
was that worst of students in any age, the ones who tell teachers they're already more expert than their instructors about a
particular topic—which often makes professors wonder: then
why are you taking this course in the first place? When you
already have all the answers, who needs questions? When you
are certain, what's the point of doubt?

Once he became bishop of Hippo (Annaba in Algeria),
Augustine turned his rhetorical skills to preaching and teaching. There is always the sense, however, that he's still pretty
sure he's right and everyone else is wrong, even as he recommends humility to counter pride. He advocated discipline and
constraint so forcefully against enemies that he wrote influential justifications for violence. Sometimes it sounds as if he's
checking himself—or maybe he's still clueless. In the letter
where he recommended humility as the three prime virtues,
Augustine was responding to a Greek man studying in North
Africa named Dioscurus. He reminds us of Augustine in his
youth. Dioscurus is in a hurry because he's about to set sail
on a trip and had written obnoxiously to Augustine requesting
quick replies to questions about Cicero so he would appear
learned to others. You can almost hear Augustine sighing as he
hears his own young self in Dioscurus's impatient letter. And
yet he starts his reply with a degree of haughtiness by chastis-
ing this man. Doesn't Dioscurus realize that a bishop like Augustine is far too busy to deal with such an impertinent request
from someone lower than a man of his importance, learning,
and tight schedule?

For when I consider how a bishop is distracted and over-wrought by the cares of his office clamoring on every side, it does not seem to me proper for him suddenly, as if deaf, to withdraw himself from all these, and devote himself to the work of expounding to a single student some unimportant questions in the *Dialogues* of Cicero.

Nevertheless, he scolds Dioscurus for being motivated by vanity:

Do you not, O Dioscorus, remember an ingenious line of your favorite Persius, in which he not only rebukes your folly, but administers to your boyish head, if you have only sense to feel it, a deserved correction, restraining your vanity with the words, "To know is nothing in your eyes unless another knows that you know."

He then counsels Dioscurus to slow down

because, unless humility precede, accompany, and follow every good action which we perform, being at once the object which we keep before our eyes, the support to which we cling, and the monitor by which we are restrained, pride wrests wholly from our hand any good work on which we are congratulating ourselves.[9]

For Augustine, pride and not money is the root of all evil. It's tied for him to original sin in the garden of Eden. Adam and Eve ate the forbidden fruit because they wanted to know what God knew. The antidote is humility, which deflates ambition and a swollen ego that put you above everyone else. Because of pride, there is no humility. You're convinced that you can't be wrong—which makes Augustine infuriating. Once he became convinced that his pursuit of fame and money was wrong, he was just as sure that his new path was correct and that now he was right about everything again, like the far-left liberal who shoots to the other end of the political spectrum and becomes a far-right conservative. As we just saw, Augustine didn't always practice what he preached. In one sermon he proclaimed, "The sum of humility for you consists in knowing yourself," which prompts Augustine and us to recall that humility can easily slip through your fingers even after it's appreciated and embraced. Humility is a habit, as is moderation, though Augustine never quite learned that second lesson.[10]

A second key figure in the medieval development of humility is Gregory the Great, who was pope from 590 to 604. Like Augustine, he was trained in the art of rhetoric and the study of philosophy. He originally pursued a standard Roman career but grew disillusioned and stepped off that track, so he was personally familiar with the dangers of pride. His decision was even more shocking than Augustine's because Gregory came from a far more prominent family and so might have risen higher and more quickly than Augustine. By the age of thirty, he held the important and influential position of prefect of the city of Rome. After about five years, he simply walked away from that powerful life, set up several monasteries with family money, and lived as a monk. That step of renouncing such high status and position strongly indicated his genuine humility. Personal witness gives credibility to his comments on humility that followed.

Gregory's skills could not be hidden: he served two popes as a legate to Constantinople for six years. When he returned to Rome, he became a papal adviser and then was elected pope—the first monk to be chosen. It appears that Gregory actively resisted every one of these church appointments and promotions because, after all, he'd resigned his civil post to live an ascetic life of study and prayer, peace and quiet. Yet in humility he also bowed to the desires and needs of others. He

was the first person to describe the pope's position as "the servant of the servants of God."

There's a revealing story about Gregory's personal humility
as pope that was preserved in both Greek and Latin manuscripts, which gives us a sense that it was worth repeating by
people who knew him in Constantinople and Rome. A holy
man with a great reputation was visiting Rome from the East.
As John the Persian was walking through the city, he saw Gregory and decided that as a sign of respect he would prostrate
himself before the pope. We'll let John narrate what occurred:
"And so when the pope came near and saw that I was going
to prostrate myself—may God be my witness, brothers—he
prostrated himself on the ground first, and did not stand up
before I had been pulled up." It's a remarkable scene: not only
does this revered pope spread himself on the ground first before this holy man, but he won't get up until the other rises.[11]

Since he was the pope, it's not surprising that Gregory
wrote about humility in theological terms: he often advised
people to follow the humility of the God who becomes human
in Jesus. For those who found a divine model unattainable,
there's also something in Gregory's words about humility that
remind us of Aristotle's recommendation that humility can
help anyone through cultivating balance. "But by wondrous
stewardship the soul is balanced at some mid-point so that it
neither takes pride in its good deeds nor falls amid evil acts,"
he preached in a homily on the prophetic book of Ezekiel in
Hebrew scripture. "Surely for God to weigh the waters by measure is to guard the perceptions of souls in humility amid good
fortune and bad, amid gifts and temptations, amid the heights
and the depths." This makes humility, powered by hope, the
mean between the extremes of pride and despair—and an appealing virtue in challenging personal times.[12]

With Gregory, as with Augustine before him and Hildegard after, we have the irony of an authoritative person

recommending humility from a high position. Like both of them, Gregory agreed that humility was the key to all the other virtues: he once called it the "mother and teacher of all virtues."[13] But in church or civil politics, pride and power threatened to go together. That combination might lead people like these three prominent and popular medieval figures to think they could go it alone: who needed advisers from either an earthly or a heavenly court?

Gregory raised this warning flag to a different Augustine, this one a bishop in England. When news reached Rome that this Augustine was converting many people by performing miracles, he wrote a letter telling him to remember that the miraculous power did not come from his own hands. Gregory told this missionary bishop to be wary of praise from others and therefore of the temptation of pride within himself:

> Wherefore you must rejoice with fear for this same heavenly gift, and tremble in rejoicing: rejoice, that is, because the souls of the English are drawn by outward miracles to inward grace. But tremble, lest among the signs that are done the infirm mind lift itself up to presumption about itself, and from being exalted in honor outwardly, fall inwardly through vain glory. . . . The mind, then, should be much kept down in the midst of signs and miracles, lest you might seek your own glory in them, and exult in private joy for your own exaltation.[14]

To his credit, Gregory was aware of this temptation in his own work. That could be why, in a commentary on the biblical book of Job titled the *Moralia in Iob*, Gregory cautions himself. Even as he's trying to do a good job preaching and teaching as pope, when he thinks later about the fancy language he used in his sermons, he realizes that he might have grown a bit full of himself. Maybe he tried too hard to draw out some applause. "For as I return to myself inwardly," he writes, "having laid aside the leaves of words and the branches of sentences, and carefully examine what I desired at its very roots, I certainly recognize that I wished most of all to please God through it; but somehow or other a desire for human praise has furtively, I do not know how, planted itself in the middle of that very desire with which I am so keen to please God."[15] In that same work, Gregory notes that it's easy to seek humility for the wrong reason and to quickly lose it in a burst of pride. Gregory paints the scenario:

> Some people, let us say, are swollen with the depraved boldness of pride, but, seeing that great esteem is accorded to humility, they rise up against themselves and cut off a growth, as it were, of intense haughtiness, proposing to display their humility against whatever insults are offered them. As soon as a single word causes a wound, however, such people immediately return to their habitual bearing of pride, and its growth continues to such an extent that they have no memory whatever of their previous desire for the profit of humility.[16]

Embracing humility is not a one-and-done action, Gregory teaches. It takes patience, practice, and persistence.

Along with Augustine of Hippo and Gregory the Great, an essential person for the medieval definition of humility was Benedict of Nursia (ca. 480–547), the founder of what is called Benedictine monasticism, from which many other orders later riffed or diverged. In his classic guide for life in monasteries and convents, he delineated twelve steps to humility. The *Rule of Saint Benedict* is quite practical and lays down nearly every aspect of the community's life: when and how to pray and work, tasks and responsibilities for daily activities like cooking and cleaning, regulations on clothing and food, and the manner of addressing wrongdoing and tensions. It's a complete manual for group living, not a guide for individuals to escape relationships.

There's a cliché that medieval nuns and monks displayed a *contemptus mundi*, demonstrating their contempt and fear of an enticing, corrosive world by fleeing it. Yes, at times medieval nuns and monks were fairly isolated and may have sought safety within closed doors in physically dangerous areas. But even within a restricted cloister, no one was alone. A successful virtuous life was the result of working with others so that the whole community could proceed in virtue. For Benedict, the key was to foster a community where humility was the North Star.

Benedict's rules applied equally to communities of women and men. The term *monastery* originally referred to a group of either men or women, but over time the word *convent* came to be associated with women's communities. The words *monk* and *nun* are more formal; early in the Middle Ages, they would have thought of themselves as sisters and brothers led by abbesses or ammas and abbots or abbas. For several centuries, neither women nor men took formal vows of poverty, chastity, and obedience, although they were in effect living in accord with these ideals. The more important promise was to stay still in one place, which became a vow of stability, and to use the community and its rule to guide progress within your own heart.

Along with male founders, women who regarded humility as key also laid the building blocks for medieval monasticism. Benedict wrote down the main plan, but men and women leaders had to make it work. The monastic heritage of humility comes not simply from Benedict, but from thousands of people over the centuries and in many cultures who struggled to embody this virtue as an animating principle in their communities. One of these very early influencers was Amma

Theodora, who led a community near Alexandria in Egypt in the fourth century CE. Her experiences made Theodora a resource for other leaders. She told one specific story to illustrate the centrality of humility. A solitary woman known as an anchorite (but who is unfortunately not named) was able to drive out demons, so naturally she asked the demons what had worked where others failed. Was it fasting? No, the demons replied, because they don't eat or drink. Vigils? No, because they don't sleep. Was it isolation from the world? No, because they also lived in the desert. So what drove demons out? The demons themselves provided the answer: they couldn't conquer her humility.[17]

Benedict's set of guiding principles and procedures wasn't original, but its genius was in synthesizing best practices. One of Benedict's most important sources was John Cassian (c. 360–453). He had a broad range of encounters with many types of people in a variety of monastic and secular settings. Born in what's now Romania, he lived in the Holy Land and Egypt, then traveled to Constantinople and Rome before settling in Marseilles, where he summarized what he'd learned in three books. In one of them, the *Institutes*, Cassian listed ten aspects of humility that a candidate for a monastic group should exhibit. They include working against self-will and being driven only by your desires; obediently acceding to elders' judgment, experience, and correction; being tolerant and even silent when someone causes an injury unjustly; and patiently moving along the path to improvement. "By such indications, and by others like them, true humility is recognized," Cassian concluded this section. "When it is possessed in truth, it will at once bring you a step higher to love, which has no fear."[18]

Cassian offered as a model a novice who was well educated and came from a rich and esteemed family, yet he didn't resist when an elder piled ten baskets on his back and sent him to a market to sell them. There was an added stipulation that would make the task take longer: if anyone wanted to buy all ten at once, he had to refuse and sell them one at a time. But he didn't protest: out he went, all day, and sold the baskets one by one.

You can teach by good examples like this one, or you can use examples of bad behavior. Cassian devoted the final book in these *Institutes* to the spirit of pride, which he said can destroy every virtue and produce every vice. He described pride as a savage beast with a cruel, poisonous bite. After recounting how Lucifer's pride caused his own fall from grace, Cassian considers how humans can learn from this epic tale to overcome pride within themselves and avoid Lucifer's fate. He gives us a few examples of how not to act. In one, he reminds us that the lack of humility can grow into the kind of pride where a person is sure he's an expert and doesn't need correction. He's quick to speak loudly and glibly but slow to listen even when the advice comes from wise elders. He's cold and thoughtless of others to the point of enjoying being cruelly abusive, but of course at the same time he's disdainful of being scolded by others. He's disobedient and impetuous, which Cassian reports as a troubling combination. A clinical therapist today would diagnose this person as a malignant narcissist. Cassian calls this kind of pride "the most pernicious and harmful lukewarmness," cautioning a few lines later that such a person "even (and this is worse) promises himself perfection based on his wretched situation and way of life." Cassian advises that one proud person such as this one, like the typical one bad apple in a bunch, can spread rot. He'll set up his own monastery and tell others what to do instead of taking advice or listening to their cautions—"a bad disciple becoming an even worse master!"

The key weapon against this kind of pride is humility. To teach his lesson, Cassian again gives us not a good example to follow but a lousy one to avoid. It seems one brother, just

starting on the monastic path, was able to control his pride
for a time and was sure that was good enough. He was willing
to get with the program, but he had his limit. When his abbot called him out for backsliding and noted that he was now
"puffed with diabolical pride," the young man "responded with
the height of arrogance: 'Must I be constantly submissive because I have humbled myself for a while?'" That left the abbot
speechless; he could only groan in sadness and shock. While
Cassian doesn't tell us what happened next, it's a safe bet that
the abbot replayed the garden of Eden and kicked the young
man out.

Benedict summed up stories and teachings like these on
humility up to the sixth century, essentially codifying them for
many later discussions of that virtue. His *Rule* is the keystone
in humility's development from the ancient to the medieval
world with a legacy for our own. Perhaps the foremost inter-
preter of that legacy is Joan Chittister, a Benedictine nun who
has written extensively on how to apply his early medieval insights to contemporary circumstances. Commenting on Benedict's emphasis on humility that she calls without reservation
the Magna Carta of this virtue, she declares: "If the twentieth
century has lost anything that needs to be rediscovered, if the
Western world has denied anything that needs to be owned, if
individuals have rejected anything that needs to be professed
again, if the preservation of the globe in the twenty-first century requires anything of the past at all, it may well be the commitment of the *Rule* of Benedict to humility."

Chittister notes that the modern world's conception of humility and Benedict's could not be further apart. She draws on
Benedict's deep psychological insights, which are reminiscent
of Thucydides's perceptive and sometimes cutting judgments
of his fellow Athenians. Me-ism—whether in Thucydides's
ancient Greece, Benedict's early medieval Italy, or Chittister's
world today—works against humility's role in binding people

together through self-knowledge and an understanding of our
need for each other. Benedict instructed medieval nuns and
monks that they needed to be humble if they hoped to form
a community where individuals and everyone could proceed
well together. Pride drove an individualism that was absolutely
opposed to the intention of a monastic community. Narcissism appears in every historical era. By contrast, Chittister
says, "The Rule of Benedict reads like a therapeutic regimen
against the illness."[19]

Benedict's Twelve Steps of Humility

Benedict outlined that therapeutic regimen in twelve steps or
stages, primarily in chapter 7 of the *Rule*, although the virtue
floats through the entire text. The language of the *Rule* can
be a bit striking: first-time readers shudder at the mention of
beating recalcitrant monks with a rod. The Latin vocabulary
is entirely masculine even though the *Rule* was from the start
applied equally to communities of women and men. For all of
its impact, the *Rule* is fairly short, running shorter than fifty
printed pages in modern editions.[20] Most of its seventy-three
chapters are one or a few paragraphs. Once a week, the nuns
and monks would gather in what came to be called the chapter
room to hear a chapter read aloud. The abbess or abbot would
then expound on some points and likely apply the message to
a particular situation taking place within the community for its
correction or progress.

Chapter 7 on humility is the longest chapter, running nearly
twenty paragraphs, which in itself is a sign of how elemental
this virtue is for the individual and community. Another sign
is that the next longest, chapter 2 on the qualities of a good
abbot or abbess, runs to about half that length. Clearly Benedict thought humility was more important to define than the
qualities of the community leader. We need to spend careful

time on these twelve steps of humility that nuns and monks should strive to climb step by step.

Drawing on Hebrew tradition, Benedict says that the first degree of humility (or step) is fear of the Lord: knowing your proper place relative to the wider world and, in Benedict's context, divinity (though his steps adapt easily to secular settings). That first step means committing yourself to avoiding vice and embracing virtue while reminding yourself that nothing is hidden. Your actions reveal your personality, your thoughts, and your core. We might call this mindfulness: being in the moment, observing and reacting to what's in front of you without self-delusion or distraction. He stresses there the danger of willfulness, of trying to impose power on what we can't or shouldn't try to control. That forceful attitude implies that we and we alone know what is best not only for ourselves but for others. Willfulness would clearly be a problem in a small and closed community where everyone is always supposed to be in a supportive relationship with their sisters and brothers. That's also true today in a business, school, political or civic association, or family. Willfulness in its worst forms can produce overbearing, heavy-handed, manipulative, or bullying behavior.

The second and third degrees of humility complement the first. In resisting your own will, be ready to follow the will of others who might know better how to act in the matter at hand. In Benedict's setting, this attitude will become obedience to the abbess, abbot, or elders in the community. Obedience strikes our modern ears as very authoritarian and antidemocratic, but Benedict's intent can still be helpful. Think of a baseball manager who has a wide-angle game plan versus one player who's only thinking of himself. The player has to unhook himself from his own self-interest and trust that the manager has the whole team's best interests in mind when making a decision or calling a play.

Benedict's fourth degree of humility is patience: "if in this obedience difficult, unfavorable, or even unjust things are imposed, they accept them with quiet patience and endure it without growing weary or seeking escape." Patience might demand swallowing criticism, whether it's offered with a bite or a hug, or adversity that could be physical or emotional. The message is that we should tough out hardships. This view might seem harsh, but you can think of this rung as steady persistence in the face of pain.

Fifth is to be honest about your faults, both actions that you took, even if you got away with them, and rotten thoughts that you had but didn't implement. There's an element of self-revelation too: don't fool yourself. The sixth degree is to be satisfied with what you have and not always look at what your neighbor has, thinking it's a better portion than yours. You have skills, they have skills. Be content with yours. The seventh is related to the prior two. It reminds us of Socrates: know yourself, principally your faults. Benedict writes this degree roughly: "they not only declare with the tongue but believe in their hearts that they are the lowest and least valuable of people, humbling themselves."

There's a challenge in the seventh degree not to replace the virtue of humility with the disordered vice of self-accusation or low self-esteem. A better way to apply this degree is to continue walking Socrates's path. Accept in a constructive way that others know more or are more skilled about something than you are. It's a reminder that there are still things for us to learn and improvements in our personalities and habits to be made. The eighth degree of humility links to the seventh but hearkens back to the second and third: the nun or monk "does nothing but what is sanctioned by the common rule of the monastery [or convent] and the example of the elders." Once again, obedience is an aspect of humility, even if we think the rules or the old way of doing things will lead to failure.

Benedict's ninth and tenth degrees of humility are hard to accept. The ninth is, in essence, "Shut up." The tenth sounds ridiculous: "Don't laugh." He cites a few biblical passages to say that too often people speak haphazardly or out of turn; it's easy to make a fool of yourself by opening your mouth. True enough. Anyone who has gone on a silent retreat knows how lovely the silence sounds. For Benedict, the intent was to keep the community largely quiet for prayer and to avoid chatter or, worse, mockery. The hum was to be contemplation, not gossip.

But there's a larger point: if we're talking or laughing, we aren't listening. A better sense of what might have been intended by Benedict's ninth and tenth rungs of humility comes from another set of regulations written not long after by Columbán, an Irish missionary in modern France, about the year 600. In his own monastic rule, Columbán stuns us with the penalty of silence or fifty lashes for anyone shouting out, or for a junior man or woman contradicting an elder. An elder, however, may correct a younger nun or monk. There is, however, a telling exception that removes the punishment of silence or lashes among equals: "If there is something more accurately true than what the speaker says and he remembers it—'If you well recollect, brother'—and the other, hearing these words, shall not affirm his own statement but shall humbly say: 'I suppose that you remember better; I have exceeded in word through forgetfulness; I repent of what I have said amiss.'" A few lines later we have the payoff that Columbán praises: "in humility of spirit each esteemed others better than himself."[21]

When you do talk, Benedict says in his eleventh degree of humility, speak softly, briefly, modestly, gently, and have something of substance to say. But actions always speak louder than words, which couples the eleventh degree to the twelfth and final one: "they are not only humble of heart but in appearance" in prayer, at work in a garden or out in the fields, or on a journey. Once the nun or monk—or any of us reading today—reaches the top of the ladder, Benedict promises that it will be natural to put others first and act charitably toward them: "all the things that at first were observed with fear, they will now begin to observe without effort, though naturally by habit." Such an ascent is the exact opposite of climbing a corporate or political ladder. Too often when that happens, ambitious colleagues start making trouble; abuse, not charity and help, flow downward.

What can we learn from this sixth-century reflection on humility, even though we aren't medieval nuns or monks? One way of answering that question is to make what might sound like an abrupt comparison, as one scholar did, between Benedict's notion of humility and the idea of sincerity found in the Chinese philosophy of Confucius (ca. 551–479 BCE). A Benedictine nun, Sister Donald Corcoran, saw in the Confucian values of sincerity or authenticity (*ch'eng*) and reverence (*ching*) links with what Benedict was trying to cultivate among his communities. She sees there shared goals of creating a serious, reverent, and mindful person. Benedictine and Confucian followers are both called to be introspective and self-monitoring—and therefore, in turn, self-correcting. Seeing both men as sages with a clear sense of how the human spirit worked, Corcoran proposes that a centering, grounded balance burns at the core of their philosophies, whether it's described as Confucius's doctrine of the mean or Benedict's monastic atmosphere of moderation.[22]

Benedict and Confucius would agree that humility is a choice that must be made consciously and practiced continually. It's a product of self-reflection and the need to submit yourself to others' insights and talents. An individual's gifts are useless if not shared, but this also entails a realization that a person has only one set of gifts and requires the talents of others. Humility acknowledges your own talents as well as your limits, recognizing that no one person knows it all, can do it all, or has it all. Humility forces us to recognize a hierarchy that is meant not to crush us or keep us down but rather to provide a ladder or path to pursue. That's obedience in a positive light, which also recognizes patience and effort as constituent elements of the path to humility. Seeing an elder's expertise prompts the young nun or monk to ask how they came by that skill or insight. Sitting at the feet of a master can turn the humble student into a sage if she realizes what she doesn't know. Once achieved, those skills are shared, which means that products of humility in a successful monastic community of medieval women and men—or groups of people working toward a common goal today—are solidarity and compassion, empathy and companionship, and hospitality.[23]

Slouching toward Humility

Even in the Middle Ages, the golden age of humility, things could go awry. Inside or outside the cloister, there is a risk of humility being done wrong. Wasn't it easy to move (or to be moved) from positive humility to degradation in the name of conquering your desires and subjecting yourself obediently to authority? It doesn't take much to turn humiliation into a supposed mark of sanctity. A well-intentioned goal can surely be exploited for power. It is one thing to practice good humility or to embrace the purgation of suffering when it came your way, but quite another to seek—or to impose—humiliation or extreme penances for yourself or others because of their alleged worth. Penitential practices intended to demonstrate your lowliness could naturally go too far.

In the twelfth century, the ascetical Humiliati movement of men and women arose from some good intentions, namely to place themselves as a corrective to worldly popes and bishops. Despite their name, their emphasis was more on living simply than proposing full-blown theories of humility in writings or rules: they put actions before words. They saw a poor church as a pure church, like the ones they read about in the earliest church documents. Reforming themselves through fasting, prayer, and service was seen as a way of trickling purgation up the hierarchy, which didn't happen. In fact, their criticisms brought excommunication in 1184.[24]

The *flagellanti* took the practice of self-imposed physical discomfort like wearing a hair shirt or a tight band of coarse cloth or metal pricks and put it on steroids. Comprised mostly of men, likely because they often marched stripped to the waist or fully naked, they tried to purge themselves of bad things like lust. They whipped themselves with lashes tipped with metal points. Many were also apocalyptic fanatics who read current events into biblical prophecies, most spectacularly in the book of Revelation with its promise of a final cataclysmic clash between the good people (which meant them) and the bad people (anyone who wasn't them). They thought the world's end was coming and that they could put off God's wrath by expiating their sins. During the Crusades and the Black Death, their mass demonstrations turned antisemitic and produced slaughters of Jewish communities. As often happens with high passions, the *flagellanti* attracted great attention in large processions but flamed out. That's performative self-destruction, even pride in self-proclaimed purity, not the virtue of humility.[25]

We find this ironic danger of excessive humility specifically in the genre of vitae (saints' lives) called hagiography.[26] There's a familiar formula to many of these vitae because hagiography is not biography in any modern academic sense. Their authors didn't gather writings, cross-check archives, and interview conflicting witnesses to tell a full, critical portrait of strengths and character flaws. The only goal was to illustrate the person's sanctity. There's a lot of whitewashing. The vitae can be far-fetched, tedious, or outright weird. It seems that many male saints spurned their mothers' breasts as infants, for example. The stories reveal some saints who endured humiliating tasks and verbal or physical abuse as well as self-mortification and penance as proof that they believed they were no better than anyone else. To conquer their self-will or self-interest, their pride or stubbornness, they sucked the pus from lepers' sores or refused to sleep with their newly married spouses. They embraced slander and torture. They stood for many days in heat or freezing water, sometimes holding their arms out in imitation of Jesus on the cross. Some slept on the ground or perched for days on columns; others walked great distances on their knees or barefoot.[27]

We have accounts of saints, more often women, who voluntarily fasted so frequently that they may have starved themselves in a phenomenon some historians have called holy anorexia. One of the most well-known is Catherine of Siena (1347–80), who was born in the year the Black Death hit Europe and lived a life of physical suffering during a period of warfare and political and social unrest. We read that once Catherine turned sixteen, she ate only bread, water, and raw vegetables, having already turned away from meat as a child. She sometimes couldn't eat bread or anything at all, though accounts of her going a month without water are not medically possible. Catherine may also have had bulimia or lasting effects of anorexia: we read that eating could upset her stomach and cause her to vomit. Other times, people saw her forcing twigs down her throat to make herself throw up. She would drink water and chew herbs, then spit them out, and described hunger as evidence of her vices of greed and gluttony. This pattern over many years must have worn her body down and contributed to her early death at thirty-three, surely from complications of two decades of self-imposed malnourishment.

At the same time, Catherine was fascinated by miraculous

legends where food appeared to feed many people in imitation
of the gospel story of Jesus feeding five thousand people with
five loaves of bread and two fish. Catherine often prepared
meals and gave away wine to her neighbors even after the
casks were empty, once cooking Sunday dinner for a family
while the mother was in church. When a woman named Alessia found that her grain was spoiled, Catherine made it fresh
again, stretched it to make more loaves of bread than it should
have, and then caused the number of loaves to keep growing.
Another anecdote has Catherine healing two women whose
breast milk had dried up; she caused the milk to flow again for
their newborns. No wonder her followers called her Mama,
and not just for her spiritual direction and example. Her enemies said her odd eating habits were a ruse to make her look
humble and weak for God. Others charged that she'd cut a deal
with the devil to survive on meager rations, which opened her
to slanderous accusations of possession and witchcraft.[28]

We can ask if Catherine took the idea of humility and self-
abasement beyond reason and safety or if that expectation
was pressed upon her. In her *Dialogue*, composed near the end
of her short life, she treats humility in many of the standard
medieval ways: a response against pride, a path to service, the
fruit of obedience and patience, a way to understand yourself.
She had done this in many letters, too, which made it an under-
current of her approach to sanctity. Like Hildegard, Catherine
combines the virtue with charity, "which is nursed and moth-
ered by humility." She urged a constant process of discernment
and self-knowledge that operated in a kind of loop with charity
and humility: "for discernment and charity are engrafted together and planted in the soil of that true humility which is
born of self-knowledge. . . . So the tree of charity is nurtured in
humility and branches out in true discernment." In a 1377 letter
to a friend and traveling companion named Felice da Massa,

Catherine reached for an accessible image to describe humility as "the governess and wet-nurse of charity."

These are positive, encouraging, and engaging images—until they're not. Later in the *Dialogue*, we read sentiments that we've come to expect, but then we're startled by troubling language:

> Every perfection and every virtue proceeds from charity. Charity is nourished by humility. And humility comes from knowledge and holy hatred of oneself, that is, of one's selfish sensuality. To attain charity you must dwell constantly in the cell of self-knowledge. . . . And you must exercise yourself in tearing out every perverse desire, whether spiritual or material, while you are hidden away within your house. . . . Then, if her love is without self-interest, she rejoices in her labors with lively faith and contempt for herself, for she considers herself unworthy of spiritual peace and quiet.[29]

Rhetorical flourishes aside, this is a disturbing indication that Catherine's quest for improvement via humility might have become a troubling perfectionism: "holy hatred of oneself . . . tearing out . . . contempt . . . unworthy." Could saints have gone overboard in purging themselves of vice and fighting against temptation to the point of deliberate self-harm? Understanding your place with respect to others and divinity makes sense from the religious concept of fear of the Lord, but having contempt for yourself can cross a line. In telling these stories as hero parables to be copied, were preachers and disciples propagating negative habits that should have been avoided as well as models to be followed?[30]

To understand humility in these saints' lives means we can't dismiss them entirely, but we've got to get past the gooey, creepy, or alarming religiosity. We've got to find the good points as well as the risks these stories had for the listener then and now. We can read the extremism of self-discipline as a cautionary tale for fundamentalism or zealotry within our own social or political crusades. There is a driving core of caring and the desire to improve a specific community that's important to us. But fighting too hard in advocating for one group of disadvantaged people can alienate other groups. Working too hard for an issue outside our home might make us overlook the people we live with and might harm our own physical or mental health. Killing ourselves for a cause isn't humble service, but fanaticism.

We shouldn't strive for humility so much that we become proud of our efforts—a funny contradiction. But it's not always funny when the issue is turned around. We shouldn't allow ourselves to be devalued and degraded, however well-meaning we might be to put someone else and their needs first. In a quest to practice humility, we might end up facilitating our own humiliation or beating ourselves up. A bit of penance and fasting is good for body and soul according to many faith traditions and meditative practices, but self-mortification takes things to another and potentially damaging level physically and psychologically. Cleaning your family's toilet can put you in your place; drinking from it can make you sick. Moderation is part of humility too.

When medieval preachers presented saints as models to follow, they had to understand that saints, being saints, were hard to imitate. We imagine a preacher offering a story of Catherine of Siena, for example, but then hopefully telling his congregation that while not everyone could (or should) go so far, perhaps they might refrain from that second cup of wine at dinner. That's the more helpful genre of an exemplum: a tale to teach, like a bedtime story or a puppet play in the town square to show children they shouldn't lie or steal or disobey their parents. These exempla were common in the medieval cheat sheets for sermons called florilegia ("little bouquets"): abstracts of snappy stories and proverbs drawn from famous sermons by big-name preachers. They give us a sense of what the average person was hearing about how to be humble in their daily lives.

One of these collections, the *Manipulus florum*, was a medieval version of *Poor Richard's Almanack* or *Bartlett's Familiar Quotations*. It has nearly one hundred entries for humility (*humilitas*) and pride (*superbia*). These entries are selections from sermons making instructive and encouraging points to the person in the pew who couldn't quite make it to sainthood. Humility is the primary shield against pride, we learn in these snippets, but it must become a habit. Humility is a teacher that helps us to bear hardships, heals us from overreaching, teaches patience and a sense of proportion, and gets easier with age and the wisdom that hopefully develops from experience. While pride closes a heart and puts itself first, humility opens hearts to serve others. Humility is angelic while pride is demonic.[31]

In the Middle Ages, a saint known for his radical personal poverty who should really be known for humility was Francis of Assisi (ca. 1181–1226). Examples from his life were staples of medieval sermons. In the medieval mind, so close was Francis to being the humble, human Jesus in their midst that he was known as an *alter Christus*—another Christ. Francis bore on his body the visible stigmata or five wounds that Jesus suffered on the cross. While we think of obedience and particularly poverty as Francis's exceptional characteristics, in his own day it was above all his humility that attracted attention and imitation. Poverty and obedience were functions of his core humility and not the other way around. For Francis, most important was the poverty of spirit that made him realize his proper place in the world—to serve others. For Francis, to follow Jesus meant walking away from status and wealth, as he'd done from his family's textile business. Pomp, praise, and pride were the enemy because they were signs of disobedience, not expressions of humility.

In his major biography of Francis titled in Latin *Legenda maior*, the head of the Franciscan order, Bonaventure (c. 1217–1274), devotes a chapter to his humility. Bonaventure begins by describing humility as "the guardian and the crowning glory of all virtue." Bonaventure says that Francis was upset when people praised him and happy to be insulted and scorned. Because he was so aware of his own sins, Francis was "careful to preserve a low opinion of himself and appear worthless in the eyes of others." Although it doesn't sound as if his eating habits were as harsh as Catherine of Siena's would be in the next century, he was rough on his own body. He ate little, suffered from stomach and eye ailments, and slept often on the ground. Some followers thought he was over the top or just too good and hard to copy. Bonaventure reports: "They knew how austere a life he led and they were deeply moved, but they made no secret of the fact that they thought his humility was rather to be admired than imitated."[32]

Francis saw obedience as evidence of humility. He saw pride as the cause of all other evils, especially disobedience. He was never a good administrator nor comfortable as a manager, so he resigned as head of his new order as soon as he could. Before he did, he worked out that its name would be the order of Friars Minor as an indication of humility for the members who were to live as the least among their communities. Their elected leader would not be called a master general as in other religious orders but a minister general charged with serving the full community, which reminds us of Gregory the Great's description of the pope as the servant of the servants of God. Francis asked for a guardian and said he'd obey him even if he was just a novice who had joined the Franciscans only an hour before. He went so far as to claim that obeying an incompetent superior was a sign of good humility at work—a challenge for anyone who's had a lousy boss.

Islamic Concepts of Humility

We shouldn't be surprised to find humility tied to obedience and service among Jews, Christians, and Muslims given their shared heritage as Abrahamic faiths. In Islam, humility (*tawāḍu'*) is allied with a praiseworthy sense of meekness and modesty within the religion's fundamental tenets of submission to Allah and patience with others. There's an underlying theme of taming your ego in order to show compassion and to serve others. Islam also offers the related concept of moderation applied to individuals and to communities, notably when faced with fundamentalism or extremism that washes out nuance and subtlety. The Islamic concept of moderation brings the breathing space to humbly encounter the ideas of other people whose positions are not our own. Once we encounter these people and positions, we should be open to understanding our indispensable dependence on each other. None of us can go it alone, and we shouldn't deceive ourselves by thinking that we can.[33]

Like the Christian Gospels, the Qur'an recommends that people pray not with ostentation but privately and humbly (Surah 7:205, 23:2). We read in this verse familiar words of service and humility knitted with generosity and patience: "The servants of the All-merciful are those who walk in the earth modestly and who, when the ignorant address them, say, 'Peace.'" (Surah 25:63). The Qur'an praises and protects the marginalized and the humble, the weak and the meek, while condemning the haughty, the arrogant, and the proud who ignore boundaries because they think they're bigger and better than others. The first set of attributes is the way to paradise, the second set is the road to hell (Surah 7:146, 39:55–63).

The best example is the story of Satan's fall. Satan, named Iblis in the Qur'an, refused to demonstrate respect for Adam along with the other angels because he believed humans were lesser beings. Full of pride (*kibr*) Iblis asserted that Allah created angels out of fire, but fashioned humans from mud. Allah wouldn't stand for it, declaring that there is no place for the arrogant in heaven, but there is a place outside for the disgraced (Surah 7:11–13). One modern commentator describes this episode as not what happened to Satan but what his pride caused to happen to him: "Poetic justice is done when he exceeds his limits. By exploding with arrogance, he imploded with humiliation."[34]

Though Islamic scholars wrote in religious terms, as with Judaism and Christianity those of another or no faith can still learn from Muslim insights. We hear echoes of Socrates's call to know ourselves in one Arabic proverb that says, "May Allah be merciful to anyone who knows the right estimate of oneself." Al-Ghazālī (ca. 1056–1111) was a Persian philosopher and mystic who spent much of his career in what is now Syria, Iraq, and Iran. In *The Beginning of Guidance*, al-Ghazālī described pride, arrogance, and boastfulness as chronic diseases of "man's consideration of himself with the eye of self-glorification and self-importance and his consideration of others with the eye of contempt. The result as regards the tongue is that he says 'I ... I ...'" In giving advice, the proud person can be cruel; when he gets advice, he rudely dismisses it. Al-Ghazālī could be quite direct, teaching at one point: "Your belief that you are better than others is sheer ignorance. Rather you ought not to look at anyone without considering that he is better than you and superior to you." There is a resonance between obedience in Islam and the Christian monastic tradition here. A youngster might be better than you because she has yet to be guilty of wrongdoing while an elder has more years of experience that trounces yours. This attitude recalls Benedict of Nursia's

ironic sixth-century advice that the wisest sister or brother in
a monastic community might not necessarily be the eldest, so
the community should have enough humility to at least listen
to the young who might have more insight.

What is al-Ghazālī's guidance on how to learn? Study with
a humble heart and mind. "If he is a scholar, you say, 'This man
has been given what I have not been given and reached what
I did not reach, and knows what I am ignorant of; then how
shall I be like him?'" In a discussion of a teacher's duties, he
said arrogant students should be pressed to realize what they
didn't know because that exercise would soften their tendency
to be boastful. Al-Ghazālī confesses that, like Augustine, he'd
been lured by the temptations of intellectual pride and arrogance, hypocrisy and envy, not only when starting his studies
but also later when praised as a learned scholar. It took time
and self-reflection for him to learn humility too.[35]

Notes

1. Dronke, *Poetic Individuality in the Middle Ages*, considers Hildegard as poet and playwright at 150–79, followed by the Latin text
of *Ordo Virtutum* at 180–92. For an introduction to the varied
aspects of Hildegard's career, see Stoudt et al., *A Companion to
Hildegard of Bingen*.

2. Hildegard of Bingen, *Scivias*, 59–61 (Declaration), 88–90 (Book
One, Vision Two, nos. 31, 33), 288 (Book Two, Vision Six, no.
100), 426 and 437 (Book Three, Vision Eight, nos. 22, 15). A
much shorter version of the battle for a human soul between the
devil and the virtues led by Humilitas that Hildegard described
in *Ordo Virtutum* is found in her *Scivias*, 529–32 (Book Three,
Vision Thirteen, no. 9). For a biography and introduction to her
works, see *Scivias*, 9–53.

3. Hildegard of Bingen, *Scivias*, 217–21 (Book Two, Vision 5, nos.
28–32), 442 (Book Three, Vision Eight, no. 18).

4. Letter 118, part 22, in Schaff, *Select Library*, I:445–46.

5. Brown, *Augustine of Hippo*, 52.

6. Augustine of Hippo, *Selected Writings*, 168–69 (*De beata vita*, 3).

7. All passages are taken from Augustine, *Confessions*, largely Book III.

8. Macqueen, "Augustine on *Superbia*," 194. For Augustine's legacy, see Groppe, "After Augustine," 191–209.

9. Letter 118, parts 2–3 and 23, in Schaff, *Select Library*, I:438–49; for Dioscurus's request, see Letter 117, I:437–38. Persius was a first-century CE Roman poet and Stoic like Seneca: Horace and Persius, *Satires and Epistles*, 138 (*Satire* I.27).

10. Augustine, *Homilies on the Gospel of John 1-40*, 444 (Sermon 25.16).

11. Phil Booth, "Gregory and the Greek East," in Neil and Dal Santo, *A Companion to Gregory the Great*, 125–26.

12. Gregory the Great, *Homilies on the Book of the Prophet Ezekiel*, 281 (Book 2, Homily 2.3). On this point, see also Straw, *Gregory the Great*, 244–48, and Demacopoulos, *Gregory the Great*, 25–28.

13. Gregory the Great, *Moral Reflections*, 34 (23.13.24). Gregory called charity the mother of virtues in a different text: Moorhead, *Gregory the Great*, 41. This reminds us of the pairing of humility and charity in one of Hildegard's visions noted earlier.

14. Letter 28, in Schaff, *Select Library*, 13.55–56. I have slightly adapted this translation to contemporary language and punctuation.

15. Gregory the Great, *Moralia in Job*, 35.20.49, as translated in Moorhead, *Gregory the Great*, 156. He issued the same warning to the preacher who might be "lifted up in private by a secret joy at his performance" and so ironically be brought down low by the temptation of pride: see Moorhead, 125–26 (*Pastoral Rule*, 4).

16. Gregory the Great, *Moral Reflections on the Book of Job*, vol. 2, 118 (7.28.34).

17. Swan, *Forgotten Desert Mothers*, 67–68; for descriptions of several women founders of early ascetic communities, see 127–49. To read some of the lives of these early medieval women leaders at greater length, see Petersen, *Handmaids of the Lord*.

18. For Cassian's recommendations and insights, see Ramsey, *John Cassian*, 93–94, 99–100 (IV.29, 39); 253–74 (XII).

19. Chittister, *Rule of Benedict*, 61–75; Chittister, *Wisdom Distilled from the Daily*, 51–66.
20. There are countless editions, translations, and commentaries. The text used here is the gender-neutral version by Sutera, *St. Benedict's Rule*.
21. McNeill and Gamer, *Medieval Handbooks of Penance*, 261 (*Regula coenobialis*, V). I have slightly edited this translation for clarity. In that last line, Columbán is referring to Paul's letter to the Philippians 2:3: "Do nothing from selfish ambition or conceit, but in humility regard others as better than yourselves."
22. Corcoran, "Benedictine Humility and Confucian 'Sincerity,'" 227–41.
23. There are many reflections on the *Rule* of widely varying quality. For those with an understanding of historical context, in addition to those of Chittister and Sutera, noted earlier, see the commentaries of Casey, *Guide to Living in the Truth*; and Latteur, "Twelve Degrees of Humility," 32–51.
24. Andrews, *Early Humiliati*, 99–135; Brasher, *Women of the Humiliati*, 91–108.
25. Dickson, "Flagellants of 1260," 227–67; Dickson, "Encounters in Medieval Revivalism," 265–93.
26. The most widespread collection of medieval saints' lives was the thirteenth-century *Golden Legend*. For a modern translation, see de Voragine, *The Golden Legend*. Others include Thomas Head, ed., *Medieval Hagiography: An Anthology* (New York: Garland, 2000); Thomas F. X. Noble and Thomas Head, eds., *Soldiers of Christ: Saints and Saints' Lives from Late Antiquity and the Early Middle Ages* (University Park, PA: Pennsylvania State University Press, 1995); and Mary-Ann Stouck, *Medieval Saints: A Reader* (Toronto: University of Toronto Press, 1998).
27. For a quantitative analysis of markers of holiness, see the statistical studies found in Donald Weinstein and Rudolph M. Bell, *Saints and Society: The Two Worlds of Western Christendom, 1000–1700* (Chicago: University of Chicago Press, 1982), 37, 155–56, 233–34 (note table 18).
28. Bynum, *Holy Feast and Holy Fast*, 165–80, 194–207; Bell, *Holy Anorexia*, 22–53.

29. Catherine of Siena, *The Dialogue*, 29, 41–42 (*Way of Perfection*, 4, 9–10); 118–20 (*The Bridge*, 63). For the letter to Felice da Massa and another, this time to an abbot, with similar imagery, see Suzanne Noffke, trans., *The Letters of Catherine of Siena*, vol. II (Tempe: Arizona Center for Medieval and Renaissance Studies, 2001), 636 and n.4.

30. Lehmijoki-Gardner, "Denial as Action," 113–26.

31. Electronic *Manipulus florum* Project, https://manipulus-project.wlu.ca/index.html.

32. Habig, *St. Francis of Assisi*, 671–79 (I.6).

33. For a comprehensive treatment of Islamic moderation that considers source material, historical applications, and modern interpretations in theory and practice, see Kamali, *Middle Path of Moderation*. See also Sophia Vasalou, "Humility in the Islamic Tradition," in Alfano et al., *Routledge Handbook of Philosophy*, 225–35.

34. Qur'an translations are taken from John Arberry, trans., *The Holy Koran* (London: George Allen and Unwin, 1953): https://corpus.quran.com/translation.jsp. For a discussion of these topics in Islamic scripture, see Jalabi, "Walking on Divine Edge," 170–88.

35. Abu Sway, "Islamic Theological Perspectives," 234; Al-Ghazālī, *The Faith and Practice*, 145–51, sections 36–38; Mohamed, "The Duties of the Teacher," I:202–3.

4

THE PARADOX OF
LEARNED IGNORANCE

The more [a person] knows that he is unknowing, the more
learned he will be.
Nicholas of Cusa, 1440

The nature of learning becomes a subject in humility's development during the High Middle Ages, about 1100 to 1350,
when universities first began and then rapidly expanded across
Europe. As a result of trade, travel, and war—including pil-
grimages and the Crusades—Muslim learning increasingly
influenced Christian scholars, sometimes through Jewish ac-
ademics who could communicate with both worlds because
they used the Semitic languages of Arabic and Hebrew as
easily as they spoke medieval French, Italian, Spanish, and
German. Teams of translators collaborated, though they came
from different faith traditions. King Alfonso X (1221–84), who
was known as El Sabio or the Wise, ordered just such a team
in Toledo to translate texts of history, astronomy, law, science,
and medicine into the everyday Castilian language. Urban European universities, which grew from cathedral schools and
were influenced by courts like Alfonso's, started in Bologna
in 1088. They were never intended to be remote ivory towers
cut off from practical questions, nor were Jewish and Muslim
centers of learning in Spain and the Middle East. A classical
curriculum was the equivalent of today's general education
courses for a college bachelor's degree. While theology was

the first core of advanced studies, over time courses in medicine and civil and religious law developed.

As al-Ghazālī had experienced, it was hard to turn your
brain or your ego off when you were bright and wanted to
understand everything, perhaps even the mysterious ways of
divinity. What was the serious medieval scholar to do? The answer is the concept of learned ignorance, grounded in intellectual humility and checking unfettered inquiry. Before we get
there, we need to understand the huge change that occurred
between studying in the monastic setting of the early Middle
Ages and the universities of the High Middle Ages, particularly
when it came to religious topics like theology. Why? Because
monastic theology in convents and monasteries had humility
baked into its very system, while scholastic theology needed
to have humility slow its breakneck pursuit of knowledge.

In the early Middle Ages, nuns and monks mostly worked
to preserve texts and did not engage many inconsistencies or
open questions. In tune with Benedict's emphasis on humility,
they deferred to the authority of the text even when it might
not make sense to them. They distrusted what they might have
characterized as semantic word games or curiosity for its own
sake. The emphasis was on a respectful and humbling engage-
ment with texts in prayer that embraced mystery. Nuns and
monks received the insights from their abbesses and abbots
while copying what they accepted as the authoritative and final say on questions from prior sages.

In sharp contrast, the new spirit of questioning in the universities turned that approach completely upside down: everything could be studied, and nothing was outside the limits
of the human mind. In the medieval university, the student
accepted the authority of the *magister* (professor), learned all
he could, then attempted to challenge that authority or push
it to its next logical step. That push was an integral part of the
process: if you weren't pressing, you weren't doing scholastic

theology. An important key was the transmission of ancient Greek philosophy to medieval Christian theology via Jewish and Islamic scholarship. Greek philosophy provided a framework for human reason and logic to explore any and all subjects with freedom and courage.[1]

Scholastic theology was fueled by scholastic humanism: not replacing divinity but using what scholars would have seen as their God-given intellectual talents to explore mysteries that had been out of bounds. If God created the world, then God was everywhere and could be uncovered. As Albert the Great (c. 1206–80) described his canvas, "The whole world is theology for us, because the heavens proclaim the glory of God."[2] Or, if you weren't a believer, then you could figure out the laws of nature by observing them. Albert was like his German predecessor Hildegard: everything fascinated him. They found interconnections wherever they looked. Like Hildegard, Albert wondered about all he observed and systematically chronicled those observations. He spent so much time walking in France, Italy, and his native Germany that his nickname was Boots. Including theology and scriptural commentary, he wrote forty volumes on zoology, mathematics, biology, botany, chemistry, metaphysics, geography, and astronomy. He is, in fact, the patron saint of scientists. He also wrote on logic and rhetoric plus politics and ethics, asking not just what we're talking about but why.

Albert wasn't one to swallow what he heard. He once tried to feed iron to an ostrich because it was commonly believed the bird had such a strong constitution that it could eat metal. This, Albert reported, was not his experience based on the experiments he conducted. Not only was he comfortable asking questions about topics that we don't normally associate with theologians, but he also wasn't afraid to seek answers anywhere they might be found, even if his sources were Greco-Roman polytheists or Jews and Muslims who didn't agree

with Christian beliefs: "In things pertaining to faith and morals, Augustine is more to be believed than the philosophers, if
they disagree. But if we're discussing medicine, I would rather
believe Galen, or Hippocrates; and if we're talking about the
nature of things, I would rather believe Aristotle or someone
else expert in natural sciences." So if a Jewish person, Muslim,
or ancient Greek had something to teach this Christian professor, so be it. Albert wasn't proud or deluded to think that only
his tradition had a monopoly on answers; he refused to cut off
any source of learning.

For people like Hildegard and Albert, if there were contradictions and conundrums in the sciences or theology, then scientific and religious truth could only be discovered by diving
into the contradictions and conundrums. The title of the most
important exercise in untangling confused rulings in church
(called canon) law makes the goal clear. Though the work is
known by the shorthand *Decretum* (1140), its author Gratian's
full title tells the story: *A Concordance of Discordant Canons*.
Robust products of scholastic probing like Gratian's replaced
the passive and conservative monastic approach of receiving
but not inquiring. In new genres, like a summa commentary
on a specific topic, medieval university scholars catalogued,
analyzed, synthesized, and summarized aspects of law, theology, and other topics in treatises that were organized more co-
herently and systematically than in monastic scriptoria.

William of Conches (ca. 1090–c. 1160), a scholar at Char-
tres, captured the spirit of the age. He resisted the notion that
a topic couldn't be studied because prior generations had put
a limit on how far the mind should contemplate that topic:
"Ignorant themselves of the forces of nature and wanting to
have company in their ignorance, they don't want people to
look into anything; they want us to believe like peasants and
not to ask the reason behind things. . . . But we say that the
reason behind everything should be sought out."[3] We also

hear this boldness, which could well be rash and lead to pride, in *Sic et Non* by Peter Abelard (1079–1142), who spent much of his troubled personal life and career in and around Paris. The whole point of this treatise titled *Yes and No* was to walk straight into questions of theology where some commentators said x and others y. Abelard's goal was to resolve the disagreement and come to a reasonable conclusion. "Indeed, by doubting we come to inquiry," he wrote about his method and intent in the prologue to *Sic et Non*, "by inquiring, we perceive truth."[4]

Abelard saw his inquiry as a humble question, not a challenge to authority. He knew what he didn't know, but he was confident he could find out. This inquiry became the standard five-step scholastic method, which was really just the scientific method applied to philosophy and theology with a healthy dose of rhetorical technique. First, you state your question (*quaestio*). To use a big one: whether (*utrum*) God exists. Second, you argue that it seems the answer is no (*videtur quod non*) and list all the arguments, reasons, evidence, and authorities supporting a negative conclusion. Third, you deliberately go against the line of inquiry you just pursued (*sed contra est*), offering counterarguments supporting an answer of yes. Fourth, you make your decisive position known by stating "I respond . . ." (*respondeo*), and last you address one by one the arguments against your position. As one scholar described this optimistic and energetic age of questioning, university professors were "alive, actively assertive, cunningly designing, storming the gates of heaven."[5]

This method made some people nervous because it could work against—or even ignore—humility. One of the most disturbed was Bernard of Clairvaux (1090–1153), an early member of the Cistercian order known also today in some places as the Trappists. It's revealing that modern scholars label Bernard the last of the fathers. He was alive during the cutting edge of this twelfth-century renaissance in learning methods, but he really belonged to that earlier monastic period that conceded to authority and was suspicious of semantics. He was old-fashioned, even fussy. While Bernard would be comfortable with the description of monastic theology as piety without learning, he was more concerned that scholastic theologians were guilty of learning without piety, an approach that would push them off pride's cliff. What Bernard wanted scholars to appreciate was the humble attitude and balancing act known as learned ignorance.

There is a caricature painting Bernard as an enemy of learning. He wasn't, but what concerned him was an unchecked exploration of knowledge for its own sake or for the glory of the author. Bernard wasn't anti-intellectual: he stridently warned that pride could easily take over discussions of topics that should be approached humbly. Was the scholar seeking insight or fame? he asked. Was cleverness outrunning proper limits? Practicing scholastic theology wasn't the problem; an excessive reliance on human effort alone was. Bernard's concern was a sterile reasoning unmoored from faith and pastoral service, which in later centuries would be labeled by the pejorative words *scholasticism* or the Latin *sophismata*. Nobody has ever discovered a manuscript where a medieval theologian asked how many angels could dance on the head of a pin or proposed a notion for every noggin, but Bernard was worried about the type of impractical thinking that too much scholastic inquiry might produce.

Could being inquisitive and speculative lead to trouble for a person's psyche or soul? Bernard feared so; Abelard and others disagreed. The scholastics claimed theirs was a faith seeking understanding (*fides quaerens intellectum*) on equal terms, which refused to relegate understanding to a secondary status. Bernard argued that Abelard audaciously relied too much on reason and risked reducing theological truth to opinion or conjecture. Inevitably, the situation led to trouble. For the last twenty years of his life, Abelard ping-ponged between teaching and condemnation. At one point, there was supposed to be a debate between Abelard and Bernard, but it turned out Abelard was just expected to stand up and be denounced. The two men were personally reconciled in Abelard's final months, which speaks to the possibility that even after many years of disagreeing, two people with very different opinions don't have to be disagreeable to each other.

Bernard was fighting a losing battle as far as the scholastic method was concerned, but it's worth diving into his ideas of humility to see how they could have been a corrective. For him, curiosity alone can lead you astray; it's rarely humble and often self-involved. Study, however, wasn't bad in and of itself, as long as the person studying understands boundaries. An example for Bernard was a theological mystery, such as the doctrine of the Trinity, which said God consists of three individual persons (Father, Son, and Holy Spirit) who nevertheless remained one divinity: $1 + 1 + 1 = 3$ but also, at the same time, $= 1$. Bernard taught that this is just the kind of idea that must be humbly accepted. He saw the confines of reason, so he called for restraint in speculation that he believed would lead you nowhere. For Bernard, the religious concept of the trinity was simply beyond comprehension because it didn't make mathematical sense in human terms. It was folly to try to figure the trinity out without faith. Bernard's position was that monastic wisdom—that is, accepting that the trinity was incomprehensible—would lead to humility. A scholastic pursuit of trying to attain understanding or knowledge of the trinity, on the other hand, would lull you into pride. You might think you solved the puzzle, Bernard would say, but you didn't. What you need to attain is learned ignorance.

Bernard, being the last of the fathers, followed Benedict of Nursia's *Rule* in advocating twelve steps. In Bernard's scenario, however, he wagged his finger against the fall to pride rather than praised the ascent to humility as Benedict had done. Writing to a fellow abbot after about ten years of experience leading monks, Bernard followed Benedict by using the image of a ladder: you descend the ladder by pride but ascend by humility. What was humility for Bernard? A bald-eyed view of yourself. Truth was the primary fruit of humility, which led to charity. Once you realize you don't have it all together, you see that you need mercy and compassion. Once you receive mercy and compassion, you'd naturally share it with others. With Hildegard and Catherine, Bernard joined humility to charity.

Bernard listed the twelve descending steps, or rungs, of pride. The first three were curiosity, levity, and giddiness. His fear was not laughter, but being flighty, moody, and distracted. Humility was serious business; acting in a silly manner caused you to fall backward, not progress forward. The next two rungs, boasting and singularity, demonstrated that a person wants to be seen as better than others. Self-conceit—the desire to be a know-it-all egotist—is another step to the depths of pride, followed by presumption that you have qualities others don't. It's not surprising to see self-justification come next; that vice gives you an out when you're sinning, committing a crime, or behaving badly. You'd then be likely to offer a hypocritical confession, the next rung down: he called it a deceitful self-accusation, an outward show of false modesty. The tenth stage is unsurprising if you've fallen this far down from the prior nine rungs: disobedience and then rebellion against your superiors.

At this point, Bernard tells his fellow abbot, it's best to toss this person from the monastery rather than infect the rest of the community because he clearly has no fear of God or any human being. Then the last two rungs inevitably proceed: with the freedom to sin comes the habit of sinning. There is only one end to this story: "The plans of his heart, the ready words of his mouth, the works of his hands, are at the service of every impulse. He has become malevolent, evil-speaking, vile. . . . The evil man who has dropped down to the bottom is ruled by evil habit, and unchecked by fear he runs boldly on to death."[6] Depressing, but hopeful too. How? For Bernard, once you understand these dangers and the ultimate price, you have a great incentive to turn the self-knowledge of your faults into a program for improvement. Having reached the bottom of the ladder, you know how to ascend it: just do the opposite virtue of all of these vices, and you will reach humility at the top. Aspiration and brutal self-contemplation provide inspiration.

How to find the right balance between faith and reason? Ask Thomas Aquinas (1225–74), who studied under Albert the Great in Paris and Cologne. Aquinas had learned from Albert an attitude of openness to insights whatever their origin, and he took Aristotle's philosophy—as it related to politics and ethics chiefly—and applied it to Christian theology. He wasn't afraid or too proud to think his faith meant others didn't have access to intellectual insights and truth. He benefited from the work of Muslim scholars like Avicenna (c. 970–1037) and Averroës (1126–98) along with Greco-Roman masters. Aquinas had helpful things to say about pride and humility as well as curiosity.

Pursuing these questions by way of scholastic theology's five steps, Aquinas placed these issues within several questions on pride, humility, modesty, studiousness, and curiosity in his *Summa Theologica*.[7] Aquinas addresses these issues in the larger context of virtue and vice, but particularly modesty. He equated moderation with a reproof to zeal, especially when tempering the drive to study with unchecked curiosity. It was Aquinas's position that humility curbs the notion that we think we can know everything. But he also advises that humility can press us to figure out what we can using reason and to understand the stopping point where reason fails. Humility puts the proper order to learning and checks pride, which can lead to disordered self-esteem. As a virtue, humility cultivates an inward disposition as opposed to an attention-seeking, external pretense as in "look at what problem I solved" or even "look how humble I am." Humility helps you to know your limits and provides a sense of proportion so you don't, like Icarus, try to fly too high and get burned.

Pride, on the other hand, pushes your thoughts about yourself and what you know out of proportion and perspective. Aquinas is concerned that you're tempted to be overconfident, overblown, and presumptuous, which reminds us of Hildegard's and Augustine's alarms against inflating your own ego and exalting yourself over others. In one spot, Aquinas writes, "Excessive self-confidence is more opposed to humility than lack of confidence is." Daring to strut is dangerous. It's safer to think a bit less of yourself than more. A drop of medicine against this illness is offered by properly ordered study that tempers curiosity, which easily falls into vanity. Aquinas applauds keenly applying an astute mind to a problem but admonishes against thinking that you can ever be a complete expert in that problem. To his credit, Aquinas understood this in his own life. He had a heavenly vision that put him in a stupor and caused him to try to burn all of his writings, which he declared to be just straw in light of what he'd experienced. He'd seen for himself the benefit of learned ignorance.

There's an interesting coda about humility to the story of Albert's mentoring of Aquinas. Dante Alighieri, in a scene of heaven in his *Paradiso*, put Aquinas at the head of a table surrounded by other big-name thinkers with Albert at Thomas's right hand.[8] The mentor sits at the right hand of the student and not the other, more traditional way around. Albert would surely have approved since he was never comfortable with high status. He was a knight's son who joined a poor order of friars called the Dominicans. He resisted being ordained a bishop, finally accepting out of obedience but resigning as head of the Regensburg diocese after two years because he just didn't feel he was doing the job well. The mentor Albert outlived the protégé Aquinas by about six years, breaking down in tears when he heard of Thomas's death. Albert, then in his seventies and poor health, still traveled to support Aquinas when some of his propositions were posthumously investigated. Years before, it was Albert who had invested in the chubby, reticent, and distant (and likely unlikable) Aquinas. He predicted that the twenty-year-old student everyone called a dumb ox would bellow teachings that the entire world would notice. So it would have been consistent with Albert's character and personal humility to accept the place Dante gave him. Sitting at his own student's right hand in paradise was just where Albert thought he should find his place card.

Pumping the Brakes

You get a sense of how much humility as learned ignorance could benefit personal and intellectual development from a University of Paris scholar named Jean Gerson (1363–1429), who as chancellor refurbished the study of theology, which he believed had lost its way. Gerson raised the same concerns as Bernard about Abelard's headstrong rush in his curriculum overhaul, published in 1402 as *Contra curiositatem studentium* (*Against the Curiosity of Scholars*). A product of a renewal of scholastic humanism, Gerson thought that speculation for its own sake had strayed from the way Plato and Aristotle envisioned study as building good citizens and public servants. There was too much *sophismata*: sophistry or self-absorbed curiosity and sterile scholasticism. Students and professors were asking complicated, impractical questions to show off and not to solve problems or help others. Full of pride and arrogance, they were playing word games. They even sought competition and contradiction with the goal of raising themselves up by knocking others down. Instead of seeking good, they sought attention. That wasn't learned ignorance. It was medieval me-ism.

Gerson wanted to subdue this zeal to increase an individual's reputation and prestige with the antidote of humility. He had two reasons. First, a good dose of self-effacement tamps down the danger of pride. Second, humility reminds the student that he's studying to serve the common good, not to inflate his ego and reputation. Too many students weren't sufficiently deferential to established answers and traditions, particularly those that were oriented toward service. Gerson was also concerned about the factionalism that can result from a lack of humility. When one group of students believed their idol, as he put it, had the brilliant answer, they didn't even listen to other voices. Their guy is right, and everybody else is wrong. This kind of pride hunts for differences and triumphs, not for points of agreement that could produce partnership. There is no room for nuance. Gerson would have appreciated the ancient Hebrew story that the students of Hillel won praise for modestly and humbly respecting the opinion of their rival students of Shammai.

Gerson described discretion as the daughter of humility. He defined discretion as an attitude that provides flexibility in your opinion—a kind of openness—and therefore the readiness to accept advice from others who know more or better than you do.[9] This is the very essence of learned ignorance. The humbler the scholar and student, the more perspective and proportion you'd gain to take the edge off your self-assurance. There should be room for doubt, which drives you to seek out the opinions and insights from people who can see further or wider than you can. Discretion counters ego and certainty. Gerson believed that discretion would check pride, which had produced vanity and striving for fame, and caused envy among faculty members and the student body. Pride also inhibited the patience he believed would help you think carefully and deeply about a topic. Pride blocked introspection and what Gerson described as "the willingness to accept counsel." When reason ran unchecked by listening to others, it naturally ran to excess, disorder, and even disobedience like "an untamed mule which ran toward every precipice."[10]

These ideas of learned ignorance come together when we look at conversations among medieval Jews, Christians, and Muslims. The very nature of faith means that a person believes what you cannot prove. Jews, Christians, and Muslims share not only a predisposition to the supernatural but also a belief in a divinity who is one and not many. Intellectual humility followed naturally: if you are entering into interreligious conversations, it's because you don't know the other person's texts, rituals, and beliefs. You have to set your own faith aside to understand the faith of the other person. This very task guards against the twin potholes of absolutism or fundamentalism and flat relativism. This kind of exchange warns against moral arrogance and a zealous superiority that your faith is the only path to salvation.

Scholars set aside religion when they knew other learned people had something to teach them—humility grounded in learned ignorance. Scholars of the three faiths regularly met in Sicily, Egypt, southern France, and the Iberian Peninsula (remember Alfonso the Wise's translation teams in Toledo). Interaction was common and at the very least implicitly respectful: why else would you go to the trouble and expense to translate someone else's text unless you knew there was value there? Even staged disputations could involve respect, if only begrudging, which is what happened in Barcelona in 1263 when Rabbi Nahmanides debated Friar Paul, a Christian converted from Judaism. The outcome was essentially a draw, though it started with a distinct advantage to the Christian, who was backed by the king. But surely casual exchanges in businesses, markets, and guilds built mutual appreciation too.

There were informal study conferences, working translation groups, and formal lectures about scripture and theology, but also (since religion could be a source of fundamental disagreement leading to conflict) about geometry, arithmetic, astronomy, geography, science, law, and medicine. The goal of engaging academically was to learn, not to beat, convert, or convince, except about the topic you were studying. We read of many examples of Jews, Christians, and Muslims studying under each other, engaging each other in public, and exchanging ideas through books and letters. The great Islamic scholar Avicenna, who influenced Aquinas, names one of his Jewish teachers as Jacob. One Jewish physician studied under a Muslim and then taught another in Tunisia. The Jewish sage Maimonides also studied under a Muslim and in turn took on another as a student. A Muslim in Damascus named Ḥasan ibn Hūd taught a text of Maimonides translated into Arabic to Jewish students. The Italian Christian philosopher Pico dell Mirandola learned Hebrew from three Jews.[11]

We might expect to find examples of denunciations of others' faith, but this happened more in the streets than in lecture halls or royal courts. Some of these interactions were indirect, such as scholars reading each other's material though they never met. But other times there were encounters, real or imagined, among scholars of some or all faiths. One example is Abelard's fictional *Dialogue between a Philosopher, a Jew, and Christian*, an earnest attempt by three people from different perspectives to understand each other. It includes this convincing definition of humility: "Humility is that whereby we refrain from the desire for empty glory, so that we don't desire to seem more than we are."[12]

These disputations could be complicated, though, and a dose of humility didn't always mean deference. You find the paradox in the work of the Catalan author Ramon Llull (c. 1232–1316), whose career demonstrates some Christian humility in dialogue with Muslims and Jews as well as an increasing insistence on proving Christians right and Muslims wrong. We start with his fictional *Book of the Gentile and the Three Wise Men* from about 1275, which Llull states he wrote for the purpose of "entering into a union with and getting to know strangers and friends." It's an amicable discussion where the Jewish, Christian, and Muslim scholars describe their overlapping beliefs so closely that it's not always clear who's speaking. At the end, they ask the gentile who'd been listening not to declare which religion he'd now choose having heard their three comments. Turning to each other, the three "took leave of one another most amiably and politely, and each asked forgiveness of the other for any disrespectful word he might have spoken against his religion."

But Llull later in his life urged military support for converting Muslims and taking the Holy Land from them. He also demonstrated more certainty than humility in a 1307 incident that he recorded as *The Disputation of Raymond the Christian and Hamar the Saracen.* Llull had traveled to what is now Bejaia in Algeria and brazenly stood up in the town square to announce he would convert to Islam if someone could convince him of that faith's superiority to his using logic and reason. Talk turned to punches, and he was thrown into prison. The Muslim Hamar visited him there to take up the challenge in conversation. Llull reports that Hamar didn't convince him to convert to Islam, though he does say, "Muslims are men well educated in philosophy and fully rational, but of the essence of God and his attributes they possess too little knowledge."[13]

The legacy of humble, learned ignorance crossed the

threshold between the medieval period and early modernity. Our guide from this chapter to the next is the German Nicholas of Cusa (1401–64), another person like Hildegard and Albert who wrote on many subjects: political theory and law, philosophy and theology, mathematics and astronomy, and interreligious dialogue. Again, like other medieval Renaissance people we've met, Cusanus (as he's known) was no ivory tower academic: he was a bishop, reformer, preacher, papal legate, and adviser, and eventually he held the high rank of cardinal.

Our concern is with Cusanus's lifelong fascination with the idea and practice of learned ignorance, which he often wrote about, directly in *On Learned Ignorance* (*De docta ignorantia*, 1440). He described the concept this way early in that treatise, where he names the influence of Socrates, Aristotle, and Augustine, among others, on his reflections about pride and humility:

> Socrates seemed to himself to know nothing except that he did not know. And the very wise Solomon maintained that all things are difficult and unexplainable in words. And a certain other man of divine spirit says that wisdom and the seat of understanding are hidden from the eyes of all the living. Even the very profound Aristotle, in his First Philosophy, asserts that in things most obvious by nature such difficulty occurs for us as for a night owl which is trying to look at the sun. Therefore, if the foregoing points are true, then since the desire in us is not in vain, assuredly we desire to know that we do not know. If we can fully attain unto this [the knowledge of our ignorance], we will attain unto learned ignorance. For a man—even one very well versed in learning—will attain unto nothing more perfect than to be found to be most learned in the ignorance which is distinctively his. The more he knows that he is unknowing, the more learned he will be.[14]

To demonstrate that learning only approximated full knowledge of a topic, Cusanus offered the image of a polygon drawn inside a circle. Our understanding of a specific topic is represented by the polygon; full knowledge of that topic is the circle. Even if it was possible to enlarge the polygon to get as close as possible to the circle, the polygon would still never be a circle. He used this drawing to stress that our understanding is always finite: we will never know all there is to know about a topic. As one scholar described the issue for Cusanus in another of his writings: "This is *docta ignorantia*, a seeing that is not seeing."[15]

For Cusanus, there is always something more to learn—a belief which should make the most advanced and accomplished expert humble. Even if we think we know all there is to know about a topic, we must admit and accept that there will be later developments which can change our minds and fill out the picture. In the early seventeenth century, Galileo saw Saturn's rings and Jupiter's moons, but in our time the Hubble telescope has seen far beyond our solar system. If Galileo declared that he'd seen all there was to see, he'd have been a fool. Learned ignorance dictates that we can only say, "this is what we can know *right now*." This attitude means that, for Cusanus and similar thinkers, knowledge can only ever be provisional; the rest is our best guesstimate or informed conjecture. We must at those times revert to metaphor, symbol, or analogy to describe what our tools and minds can't yet comprehend. In another work called the *Hunt for Wisdom* (*De venatione sapientiae*, 1463), Cusanus did just this by saying a philosopher is like a hunter walking through a field tracking his prey. Whenever he catches something to cook and eat that satisfies him, he still must keep searching because he's learned from experience that tomorrow he'll be hungry again. Cusanus put it this way in another passage from *De docta ignorantia*: "Therefore, it is fitting that we be learned-in-ignorance beyond our understanding, so that (though not grasping the truth precisely as it is) we may at least be led to seeing that there is a precise truth which we cannot now comprehend."[16]

We must also admit that our descriptions of what we know so far and our conjectures (even as they become ever more informed) are conditioned by our own biases, experiences, prejudices, limits, languages, and judgments. The medieval legacy of learned ignorance pushes us to intellectual humility. We should get more comfortable with our incomplete knowledge because we know that part of learning is admitting that we'll never have complete knowledge. In the modern world, however, there is more of a rush toward a completeness not tempered by the humility our medieval guides recommended. Humility drops back to humiliation in the coming centuries, but it remains an important standard and one worth recovering.

Notes

1. For a comparison of monastic and scholastic theology in intent and methodology, see Leclercq, "The Renewal of Theology," 68–87.

2. For this and what follows, see McGinn, *Doctors of the Church*, 115–18. The quotations are from Albert's commentary on the gospel of Matthew (13.35) and Peter Lombard's *Sentences* (II Sent., d.13, a.2). For studies of the stunning breadth of his learning and his open-mindedness to other traditions, see Resnick, *A Companion to Albert the Great*.

3. Quoted in Chenu, *Nature, Man, and Society*, 11.

4. Abelard, *Peter Abailard*, 103. For Abelard and Heloise's relationship, including Abelard's own version in his *Historia calamitatum* (*Story of My Misfortunes*), see Abelard and Heloise, *Letters of Abelard and Heloise*.

5. Trinkaus, *In Our Image and Likeness*, vol. 1, xxi.

6. Bernard of Clairvaux, *Steps of Humility*; Sommerfeldt, *Spiritual Teachings of Bernard of Clairvaux*, 53–88.

7. Aquinas, *Summa Theologica*, 2a–2ae, questions 160–62 and 166–67.

8. Dante, *Divine Comedy*, "Paradiso," canto 10.

9. *De distinctione verarum visionum a falsis* (*On distinguishing true from false revelations*, 1402), 4; Boland, "Concept of Discretio Spirituum," 86–87; McGuire, *Jean Gerson: Early Works*, 343.

10. Pascoe, *Jean Gerson*, 99–109; McGuire, *Jean Gerson and the Last Medieval Reformation*, 134–36; Burrows, *Jean Gerson*, 243–56.

11. Glick, "'My Master, the Jew,'" 157–82.

12. Abelard, *Ethical Writings*, 118.

13. Gregory Stone, "Ramon Llull and Islam," in Austin and Johnston, *A Companion to Ramon Llull*, 120–25; Annemarie C. Mayer, "Llull and Inter-Faith Dialogue," in Austin and Johnston, *A Companion to Ramon Llull*, 156–62.

14. Nicholas of Cusa, *On Learned Ignorance*, 6 (I.1.4). For Augustine's influence, see Dubbelman, "I Know That I Do Not Know," 460–82.

15. McGinn, "Seeing and Not Seeing," 47.

16. Nicholas of Cusa, *On Learned Ignorance*, 58 (II.1.90).

5

MODERNITY FORGETS—AND
STARTS TO REMEMBER

My name is Ozymandias, King of Kings;
Look on my Works, ye Mighty, and despair!
Nothing beside remains. Round the decay
Of that colossal Wreck, boundless and bare
The lone and level sands stretch far away.
  Percy Bysshe Shelley, 1818

You might remember the scene from the 1993 Steven Spielberg movie *Jurassic Park*: John Hammond, the gazillionaire visionary behind the project to grow extinct creatures from ancient DNA, opens his dinosaur dreamland without considering the consequences. Looking for approval and legitimacy—and of course praise and eventually profit—he summons expert consultants to his laboratory island. They aren't buying it. They point out that Hammond and his scientists disregarded what they didn't know. Their DNA sequence for the dinosaurs fell short, so they substituted frog DNA. What could go wrong?

The critic who hits the central issue hardest is Dr. Ian Malcolm, an expert in chaos theory. Skeptical from the very beginning, he issues a dark observation. "The lack of humility before nature displayed here staggers me," says Dr. Malcolm. Hammond is disappointed and defensive: his achievement isn't being respected or appreciated; his scientists aren't being given their due. Malcolm calls him out: "Yeah, but your scientists were so preoccupied with whether or not they *could* they didn't stop to think if they *should*." In the end, like a true ancient Greek or Shakespearean tragedy, Hammond's own arrogance ends up throwing himself, his team, and his own grandchildren to predators running wild.

In the modern period, humility and hubris battle each other as learned ignorance was pushed aside after the Middle Ages. It's a nuanced, complicated story that resists clichés, as it should. Even as some tried to stem the tide of arrogance, we run into the sense that caution and limits were counter to the restless, optimistic, but also sometimes blind spirit of the age that could blow past the guardrails of humility. Thinkers and inventors in the Enlightenment and Scientific Revolution were not thoughtless automatons or mad scientists with no hearts: some wrestled with the medieval balance of faith and reason, but others did push their fields' envelopes without stopping to think much about ramifications. Romantic authors and painters raised concerns about the arrogance of thinking we could figure out everything. Nationalism could lead to both proper pride in your culture as well as arrogance that your superiority could justify repression and atrocity. In this chapter, we track how modernity tended to overlook humility, but we also discover that some people saw the consequences of forgetting humility and called for a rediscovery of a lost virtue.

Humility in a Time of Change

Though there was no remote control that clicked on the Renaissance, change accelerated around the globe as the Middle Ages grew into the time period we call early modernity. Chinese explorer Zheng He (ca. 1371–1433) opened sea routes to Indonesia, India, the Middle East, and Africa. Columbus crossed the Atlantic in 1492. Martin Luther asked fundamental questions about authority in 1517. On November 8, 1519 (it was a Saturday), Aztec emperor Montezuma met Hernando Cortés at Tenochtitlán, today's Mexico City, in an event that instantly doubled the known world for both societies. Change was in the air in this age of exploration and encounter, but also, and inevitably, so were conflict and competition. Humility was not considered an asset for the adventurous.

Yet just at this moment, two mystics in Spain tried to offer checks to unfettered optimism about progress by discussing humility in sophisticated ways. The first was Teresa of Ávila (1515–82), an abbess who, like Hildegard, was a formidable reformer. She's an important Carmelite nun for many reasons, but we're concerned here with her ideas of humility in this transformative century when her native Spain was grabbing property and people in the Caribbean and Latin America.[1] Teresa, even though she was schooled in the monastic tradition of humility, held a complicated view of the virtue, particularly in terms of the gendered church politics of her life. She considered humility a potentially dangerous and suspect virtue that, in the wrong hands and circumstances, could end up enslaving and not liberating a person. She was not going to let that happen to her or her nuns.

Teresa's skepticism about humility is a bridge between the Middle Ages and early modernity. Her ideas challenged the monastic notion of humility as quiet obedience and ennobling suffering. Dispatched wrongly, Teresa said, humility could lead to letting yourself be walked over. A manipulative abbess or abbot, exercising authority over nuns and monks, could abuse the idea of humility by presenting it as a passive virtue. That is why self-knowledge is so critical to Teresa: it helps a person find the proper range of humility as it sits appropriately between hubris and humiliation along the line of Aristotle's spectrum. Both poles were a temptation for Teresa, just as they had been for Hildegard, since Teresa was peppered with criticism by male civil and religious authority figures, including in the Office of the Inquisition, for her powerful influence and mystical visions.

Teresa wrote her masterpiece, *The Interior Castle*, in 1577. In treating what she calls the first dwelling place, she strongly recommends self-knowledge. The room of self-knowledge, which Teresa labels the right road, should be your first stop. As you travel through the castle (a kind of personal memory palace) you shouldn't linger in any one room too long unless it is that specific room of self-knowledge, which she immediately links to humility: "For humility, like the bee making honey in the beehive, is always at work. Without it, everything goes wrong. . . . While we are on this earth nothing is more important to us than humility." The humility that comes from self-knowledge is an attitude that makes you realize who and what you are and aren't, but also compels you to find out more: it dispels fear and powers insight. You know you're not expert in everything and can't control all circumstances, but you're also confident in what you do know and should do. In this sense, Teresa's concept of humility cultivates bravery and persistence.

Teresa gives notice that humility can be employed by enemies to make you feel small and isolated or to demean your abilities. That's false humility and leads to self-delusion, which produces inner turmoil. It's not healthy self-knowledge, which you will know is authentic because it provides a sense of peace. In her own life, knowing who she was and wasn't allowed her to push back against her opponents who saw her reform efforts and visions as disruptive, particularly for a woman. As the theologian Lisa Fullam described her efforts, "Humility can indeed be a weapon used by wicked people to oppress the powerless, but Teresa, set loose by humility and the courage that goes with it, turned this weapon against them."[2] It takes guts to tell people to slow down, to think, and to stop trying to control everything and everyone. Because of a proper sense of humility and its role in her life and leadership, Teresa had guts.

Ignatius of Loyola (1491–1556), our second mystic, grew up in the fiercely independent Basque region of Spain. He spent the first part of his life deliberately embracing pride, arrogance, and hubris. Born to well-off nobility, he was named Iñigo and later changed his name to Ignatius after a life-changing injury that opened his eyes and eventually led him to establish the Society of Jesus, called the Jesuits, with some companions in 1540. Before that catastrophic wound and its barbaric aftermath, he was the youngest son who needed to prove himself. He was brought up as a courtier and young knight in influential circles. In his twenties, Iñigo visited the royal court of King Ferdinand II of Aragon, the widower of Queen Isabella I of Castile who had financed Columbus's voyages.

The young Iñigo's loves were the standard wine, women, song, brawling and gambling, and glory in battle stirred up by troubadours' stories of chivalry and adventure. In his sixties, he dictated an autobiography in Spanish where he referred to himself in the third person: "Up to the age of twenty-six he was a man given to the follies of the world; and what he enjoyed most was exercise with arms, having a great and foolish desire to win fame." He was thick-headed, even after his major life refocus. Later in his career, it was reported that once he had decided, he couldn't be persuaded to change his mind. As a cardinal in Rome said, "He has already driven in the nail." Before he came to prominence as a knight and then religious leader, his aunt María saw through his stubbornness. "Iñigo," she told him, "you'll never learn sense until someone breaks one of your legs."

That's exactly what happened. In a spectacular example of the downside of the pursuit of pride, Iñigo led an idiotic attempt in May 1521 to defend Pamplona, with incomplete fortifications, against French forces that vastly outnumbered his—perhaps up to ten to one. His own brother took one look at the odds and ran away. The kid brother, as always craving attention and stardom, galloped straight ahead. Iñigo would not be shamed into surrender; in fact, he probably imagined a chance for celebrity beyond the grave if he was killed. Writing about thirty years later, the now-revered Jesuit leader and mystic couldn't refrain from remembering (still with a bit of ego?) that his comrades at Pamplona "drew courage from his spirit and determination."

As it turned out, a cannonball ripped between Iñigo's legs, shattering one and damaging the other. Treated at the scene by the French, who honored his valor and released him about two weeks later, he was eventually brought home to Loyola. There was a poor attempt to reconstruct the legs, which he described as butchery. Recall that we are centuries away from anesthesia, but he reported that he didn't cry out or grimace and only tightly clenched his fists. After being touch and go for a time, Iñigo noticed his right leg had healed improperly and was now shorter than the left. A bone had knit to overlap another, leaving an unsightly bump that would make his legs unattractive in fashionably tight hose and boots—"an ugly business" that would hurt his worldly rise: "He could not bear such a thing because he was set on a worldly career and thought that this would deform him." The doctors said the operation would hurt tremendously and be followed by a painful convalescence of stretching the bone. Iñigo ordered the surgeon to rebreak the leg and saw the bump away.

Sometimes it takes a cannonball to wake you up. In this case, just as his aunt María had predicted, that broken leg knocked sense into him. It forced Iñigo to see what pride had produced. As he lay in bed for weeks and then months while his leg was being stretched, he asked to read the familiar books of chivalry he'd loved as a youth that had inspired his ambition for worldly fame. None were around, so someone handed him a life of Jesus and a book on the saints translated into Castilian: these books unexpectedly engaged him. They made him ask: what if I lived my life humbly for others with the same fervor that I've been living my life proudly for myself? This episode changed Iñigo's life, but it took years to turn from the vice of hubris to the virtue of humility. Sometimes humility can be learned and then grow into habit only over quite some time and with dedicated practice. Iñigo had to start from scratch. A lifelong limp was a daily memento of where his arrogance had led.

An important moment in his development came when he spent about a year in Manresa, a town in Catalonia. He was just past his thirtieth birthday and floundering so much about what was next that he even thought about suicide. He didn't have the tools to process his flurry of emotions and thoughts. One day he went for a walk and sat down on the banks of the river Cardoner, where he was hit with an "outstanding illumination" that filled him with gratitude. Dictating this story decades later, he didn't go into specifics but said he learned more in that moment than he would the rest of his life. Looking at what happened next, it's clear part of the illumination must have been the realization he needed help. He had to humble himself to accept his ignorance about the new path. The former chivalrous knight had to be taught like a child. The life of service he envisioned after the cannonball meant the world would no longer revolve around him. It's not about me, it's about you.

Other lessons followed. He realized he needed to learn Latin to pursue the higher education necessary for his new life of service. This makes Iñigo a hero of adult learners. His education in letters had not been up to the same level as his training in arms, so at the age of thirty-three the disabled war veteran squeezed onto a bench with boys, like a parent today squishing into a third grader's desk at parent-teacher night. There, in what we'd call an elementary school in Barcelona, he started Latin 101, conjugating verbs and declining nouns with young boys likely wondering what he was doing there. The age difference and plodding experience with grammar lessons must have been a step up the ladder of this newfound but still foreign virtue called humility.[3]

Over time he began to see that service was not humiliating but dignified. To serve the poor, he had to be poor. What he sought, in a Spanish expression, was *humilidad amorosa*: a loving humility honed by practice that developed into habit for the right reasons. Humility taught him to be giving, which he hadn't been, and not grasping, which he had. That habit was cultivated by obedience, which he found checked his pride. In turn, he appreciated that humility led him to revere and respect the opinions and skills of others. He needed lots of help, and he learned to ask for it with eagerness and not begrudgingly. After all, he was a complete novice in the worlds of learning, service, and spirituality. Even after years of progress, he recorded a prayer in his diary on Palm Sunday 1544: "Give me loving humility, and with it reverence and affectionate awe."[4]

Ignatius, who had taken up this name after he moved to Paris for advanced studies in his late thirties, had long been keeping a journal of the insights he received in prayer and his thoughts and feelings about these experiences. He used these notes to offer retreats for men, some of whom became the first Jesuits, and women, many of whom became indispensable in financing his efforts. At some point, he gathered these notes together into what are called his *Spiritual Exercises*, not a book to be read leisurely but a manual for the director of a retreat. Such retreats typically last for thirty days of prayer and thought. Jesuits experience the full thirty days twice in their careers: during their two-year novitiate and then right before pronouncing their final vows about a decade later. There are shorter adaptations of three, five, and eight days or for daily use. Even if you are not religious, the *Spiritual Exercises* can be used as a method to think through decisions, and its techniques have remained popular with counselors and lay people ever since Ignatius first developed them. He called this a process of discerning intellectually and emotionally among several different courses of action by exploring their potential impact on you and others.

Ignatius identified what he termed three degrees of being lovingly humble in the second week of the *Spiritual Exercises*. In the first degree (and using his religious context), you follow God's law in order to make good, moral decisions and therefore always be in a right and positive relationship with divinity and humanity. Think of it as a kind of voluntary moral or ethical obedience to a code or standard of living that can be religious or not depending on your beliefs. The law he mentions can be divine or civil.

The second degree of humility is to be open to whatever comes your way. This is often called "indifference," but that doesn't imply a bland ambivalence toward one way or the other—chocolate or vanilla, it doesn't matter, whatever. For Ignatius, indifference means that you deliberately detach yourself from improper, self-absorbed, selfish desires that put you first totally and always. It's a way of turning around "me first, you second" to "you first": I'll do whatever helps you. You can think of it as accepting the situation in which you find yourself, all things being about equal, and doing your best within that position. He's not saying that ambition to do better and to improve yourself is bad, but that drive can be debilitating if it's nothing but unchecked and self-absorbed ambition. Ignatius's concept of indifference has the Socratic sense of being content with knowing what you can and can't do as well as being open to other people's ideas about yourself and the best use of your talents for the good of a community. You express your wishes but go where you're sent.

The third degree of humility, which he says is the most perfect, and so is the hardest to achieve, is that you explicitly, purposefully, and regularly choose the right path instead of simply submitting in obedience to another person's authority or being indifferent, though both are fine attributes. It's an equation: the first plus the second degrees of humility equal the third and highest level. You choose openness and service freely as an attitude and a habit rather than degrading yourself in humiliation or looking for praise.[5]

Now, you might say Ignatius is just too much; he's spiraling toward humiliation, even self-humiliation, as in thinking too little of yourself. But when you put Ignatius's three degrees in line with the development of humility that we've been tracking, you see what he is after. The goals are in line with the better aspects of humility as a virtue. You understand your place and your skills. You don't live in delusion. You choose to avoid the dangers of pride and arrogance by cultivating the habit of humility through practice and by consciously learning from others.

It's very easy to dismiss Ignatius as a religious militant with a psychological self-esteem problem: who would choose (or even just accept) poverty and contempt? When you read how Ignatius acted in the twenty years between his wounds and the time when he and his first companions established the Jesuits, you notice that he tends to extremes, but they mitigate gradually after Manresa. Ignatius's early penchant toward fanaticism, like Catherine of Siena's eating habits, can easily turn you off: this person is compulsive. He's gone from one extreme to the other, from arrogant knight to downtrodden beggar. He fasts too often and eats poorly to the point of giving himself stomach ailments. He sleeps outside and in rags. When he's not barefoot he cuts a hole in his sandals to wear them down more quickly. It's like he's trying to prove himself to himself. "I was going to be the best knight," you can hear him saying in his head, "but now I'll be the best saint. Watch me." You want to say: lighten up. That's not humility; it's stupid and maybe even prideful playacting.

But because he was open to learning about humility from

others who knew more about the type of service and education he intended, he learned to modify his habits to serve a larger purpose—an example of humility resulting in perspective and moderation. When he was studying in Barcelona and then in Paris, he found that fasting made him dizzy and messed up his study habits. He allowed himself to daydream about spiritual matters when he should have been paying attention in class. Ignatius saw that something was wrong, so he decided to seek out people who knew better, like scholars and masters of prayer. He understood that he was there to learn. There's a time for prayer, they told him, but it's not during a lecture. If fasting too much harms your health and your sleeping, then it's interfering with studying, which is your primary job here and now. So dial down on the fasting. And so he did. Humility gave Iñigo the courage and confidence to become Ignatius.

When you read Teresa and Ignatius on humility in the middle of the sixteenth century, you get the sense they feel the virtue of humility is slipping away. They're trying to hold on to the virtue as Roman Catholicism was losing its monopoly on Christianity. Even a Protestant leader like John Calvin (1509–64), writing in Geneva about the same time as Teresa and Ignatius, was fully in line with the medieval tradition of intellectual humility. While disagreeing with many points of Catholic theology, Calvin still embraced the limits of understanding that had been a part of the medieval golden age. "And let us not be ashamed," Calvin wrote in his *Institutes of Christian Religion* when addressing the notion of predestination, "to be ignorant of something in this matter, wherein there is a certain learned ignorance."[6]

Still, if you think people such as these are fighting a rearguard action against humility's fall, you're onto something. Contrast Teresa, Ignatius, and Calvin with their contemporary, Dutch humanist Erasmus (ca. 1467–1536), who adopted the Latin phrase *Concedo nulli* as his motto, which later appeared on seals and medals with his portrait. It can be translated as "I concede to nobody" or "I yield to nobody." Though later in life he said its meaning was connected to the Roman god Terminus to indicate that death cannot be resisted permanently, Erasmus's sharply critical personality and know-it-all strut are certainly captured by the phrase that, for our purposes, embodies the rising arrogance of his age. The slogan is a brash chin stuck out confidently to take on all comers. Nothing and nobody was going to hold back Erasmus or the emerging early modern world of rapid change.

The Scientific Revolution and Enlightenment

The scientific revolution was about collecting, cataloguing, summarizing and, in a sense, trying to control the natural world—a concern and result that made Jurassic Park's consultants nervous. The move was toward uncovering scientific facts via a systematic method of rational inquiry driven by human observation and experimentation in place of waiting for revealed dogma. True, we saw medieval figures that we can call scientists in some modern sense, like Hildegard of Bingen, Albert the Great, Averroës, Avicenna, and Maimonides.

But these medieval figures recognized limits to what they could know—and here's the really important part: they were comfortable with those limits. They knew that the unknowable was always beyond their grasp. The historian of culture and ideas Caroline Walker Bynum said that medieval people were simply more at ease with a sense of what can't be known because of an inherent comfort level with the concept of wonder. It's not that they didn't ask why, but that they realized there was not always an answer to that question. The category of wonder was something to be cherished, not explained away. Embracing wonder was an exercise in intellectual humility.[7] The difference in the early modern period is that those

medieval limits and sense of awe did not always exist. For early
modern people, it's not that we shouldn't know certain things.
We just don't know them yet, an attitude that made intellectual humility and learned ignorance a flaw or an excuse and
certainly not a virtue.

British scientist Francis Bacon (1561–1626) used the in-
ductive method to move from the particular observations he
made to drawing general conclusions. René Descartes (1596–
1650) saw mathematics behind everything but flipped Bacon
upside down: his deductive method moved from the general
to the particular, breaking things into their component parts
and first principles. For both, everything could ultimately be
understood. Descartes believed that everything came down to
mind and matter: mind can fully understand matter, and matter was controlled by motion. His *Discourse on Method* (1637)
described four steps in what he called long chains of reasoning.
First, accept nothing as true that is not known to be true. This
attitude moves from skepticism to certainty and avoids ideas
that collapse if an initial step is false. Second and third, divide
questions into parts and arrange them logically to move from
simple to complex answers. These steps remind us of Aquinas
and the scholastic method. Finally, be thorough and comprehensive; leave nothing out. From these steps flowed advances
in biology and chemistry: Robert Boyle (1627–91) codified
laws of chemistry while Swede Carl Linnaeus (1707–78) clas-
sified plants and animals. A series of physicians used the pre-
viously frowned-upon method of cutting into cadavers. They
now could understand that the human body was an organism
of interconnected systems of blood circulation and organs,
bones and tendons, muscles and joints.

Some saw the limits of their own methods and findings.
Charles Darwin (1809–82) knew his work on evolution was
part of a process of discovery. In the introduction to *Origin of
Species* he made just this point:

This Abstract, which I now publish, must necessarily be imperfect. I cannot here give references and authorities for my several statements; and I must trust to the reader reposing some confidence in my accuracy. No doubt errors will have crept in, though I hope I have always been cautious in trusting to good authorities alone. I can here give only the general conclusions at which I have arrived, with a few facts in illustration, but which, I hope, in most cases will suffice. No one can feel more sensible than I do of the necessity of hereafter publishing in detail all the facts, with references, on which my conclusions have been grounded; and I hope in a future work to do this. For I am well aware that scarcely a single point is discussed in this volume on which facts cannot be adduced, often apparently leading to conclusions directly opposite to those at which I have arrived. A fair result can be obtained only by fully stating and balancing the facts and arguments on both sides of each question; and this cannot possibly be here done.[8]

For Darwin, steps in the scientific method would always be just that—steps. His own book, he knew, was the beginning of a conversation, not the end, and he certainly knew it wasn't the last word on the subject.

The Enlightenment, which flourished in the eighteenth century, was named for its claim to rescue modernity from supposedly medieval darkness and superstition. Many *philosophes* (as some of the proponents of Enlightenment thought were called) saw themselves as reformers who wanted to use their ideas as catalysts for social change. Like their scientist colleagues, they valued reason over revelation. Not all were antireligious, but many were deists: there was a sort of impersonal creator God, likely just one, who built the world like a watch or a clock, to use Newton's familiar image. Once it was wound, the intelligible world moved along without divine intervention. Humans—this meant free white men of property to them—could determine their own political, social, and economic lives. These beliefs led authors such as Thomas Hobbes (1588–1679), John Locke (1632–1704), Baron de Montesquieu (1689–1755), Jean-Jacques Rousseau (1712–78), and Adam Smith (1723–90) to write about representative government, natural law, education, and unfettered community participation in civic and business life. Their optimistic perspectives were marked by a certain confidence that humans could achieve what they wanted without many limits. Humans were in control of their fate and consequences.

A good example of their attitude comes from the Scottish philosopher David Hume (1711–76), who is sometimes labeled a skeptic and was a writer known for a stylish and uncompromising pen. Hume was no fan of humility. Perhaps we could excuse these absolute and completely dismissive words from early in his career, given the typical hubris of a young man trying to establish his name in his field: "Every valuable quality of the mind, whether of the imagination, judgment, memory or disposition; wit, good-sense, learning, courage, justice, integrity; all these are the causes of pride; and their opposites of humility," Hume wrote in *A Treatise on Human Nature* (1739–40). "Pride produces pleasure; humility produces pain. . . . Humility is shame, not satisfaction, of our looks, skills, positions, and accomplishments."

This was not just youthful, brash disdain, however. Hume was just getting started. In his *An Enquiry concerning the Principles of Morals* (1748) he really pummels the Middle Ages as a time of monkish virtues in contrast to his own enlightened century.

> Celibacy, fasting, penance, mortification, self-denial, humility, silence, solitude, and the whole train of monkish virtues;
> for what reason are they everywhere rejected by men of

sense, but because they serve to no manner of purpose; neither advance a man's fortune in the world, nor render him a
more valuable member of society; neither qualify him for the
entertainment of company, nor increase his power of self-
enjoyment? We observe, on the contrary, that they cross all
these desirable ends; stupify the understanding and harden
the heart, obscure the fancy and sour the temper. We justly,
therefore, transfer them to the opposite column, and place
them in the catalogue of vices.

Hume scoffs here at humility as well as at most other virtues,
labeling them instead as vices that hold people back from
pleasure, power, and progress. From this perspective, humility
restrained progress and modern developments—the democratic institutions, pluralism, and tolerance that Enlightenment thinkers valued. But there is another way to look at the
matter: what could make a person more open to the ideas of
others than a humble attitude that your (and your culture's)
answers to questions about government, law, and order might
not be the only ones, let alone the best ones?

Hume was not alone in slandering the Middle Ages for a
supposed slavish dependence on monarchy backed by religious authority and blind faith. In his six-volume *History of the
Decline and Fall of the Roman Empire* (1776–88), British historian Edward Gibbon (1737–94) repeatedly labeled Christianity as superstitious and monkish, negative qualities that he
contended had weakened and destroyed his beloved Roman
empire. Hume and Gibbon discounted the role religion played
in cultivating a proper sense of humility. Hume in particular
fundamentally misunderstood the concept of fear of the Lord
from the monotheistic tradition. We turn for evidence to his
*Dialogues concerning Natural Religion and the Natural History
of Religion*, published three years after his death: "Where the
deity is represented as infinitely superior to mankind, this

belief, though altogether just, is apt, when joined with superstitious terrors, to sink the human mind into the lowest submission and abasement, and to represent the monkish virtues
of mortification, penance, humility, and passive suffering, as
the only qualities which are acceptable to him."[9] Hume stands
as the prototypically arrogant Enlightenment philosopher. Everything is up to the human brain so there should be no con-
straints. Anything that stands in the way of progress is a vice,
not a virtue. There is no place for humility in this scenario: it
crushes you and makes you crush yourself.[10]

Enlightenment goals and scientific innovations helped to
produce the Industrial Revolution, which began in the eighteenth century and took off in the nineteenth. Inventors and
entrepreneurs remade the process of gathering raw materials,
manufacturing them, and trading around the globe. In the process, cataclysmic damage was done to the environment and to
the condition of workers in the quest to increase production
by great multiples as quickly as possible. The major shift from
an agricultural to a manufacturing economy also remade our
relationship with work, leisure, and even time itself. There was
a cycle spinning ever more quickly: more goods, more labor,
more consumers in an endless loop.

Invigorated by Enlightenment optimism and technological
advances, popular opinion praised and rewarded the entre-
preneurial pursuit of wealth. New mechanized equipment, including the cotton gin, spinning jenny, railroads, and modern
factories along with steam power and hydraulic energy helped
owners make more goods. Standards of living for some people rose dramatically at the same time that politics insured
profit at the expense of workers. The stunning arrogance of
the age is captured by a remark Prince Albert, Queen Victo-
ria's husband, made in London in 1849 as the Crystal Palace
Exhibition was being constructed. The exhibition's goal was

to demonstrate British technological advances to the world. It was an exercise in bragging to other nations and even history: "Man is approaching a more complete fulfillment of that great and sacred mission which he has to perform in this world," Prince Albert declared, "to conquer nature to his use."[11]

Warnings about Forgetting

Not all early modern scientists, *philosophes*, and artists forgot humility. Those who didn't wanted people to understand the consequences of forgetting. The German philosopher Immanuel Kant (1724–1804) is more judicious and fairer to humility as a virtue and positive personal quality than Hume. In the second part of his *Metaphysics on Morals*, entitled "Doctrine of Virtue" (1797), Kant makes clear that it's very easy to get humility wrong. If you think humility means comparing yourself favorably to someone else, no, that's ambition. If it's comparing yourself unfavorably to another person, that's also wrong. There, you're being self-defeating. We have, Kant directs, a duty to others that ambition would prevent because ambition connotes competition: the goal of ambition is to be better than another, to win, to beat, to demonstrate superiority. On the other side of the ledger, we also have a duty to ourselves, which would be harmed by false humility or self-degradation. His answer?

> True humility follows unavoidably from our sincere and exact comparison of ourselves with the moral law (its holiness and strictness). But from our capacity for internal lawgiving and from the (natural) human being's feeling himself compelled to revere the (moral) human being within his own person, at the same time there comes *exaltation* and the highest self-esteem, the feeling of his inner worth, in terms

of which he is above any price and possesses an inalienable dignity, which instills in him respect for himself.[12]

Hume would not have agreed.

Notice that while Kant offers a place for a religious understanding of humility by speaking of moral law and holiness, he also says there's room for thinking about humility outside the language of religion. Natural law and conscience dictate proper self-respect and self-esteem, too. For Kant, humility is still a virtue, even in his enlightened age, and you don't need to be religious to appreciate it. Humility entails a healthy self-knowledge. It balances strengths and weaknesses and leads to the chance for self-improvement and opportunities to learn from others. Humility requires courage and honesty because it's an elemental view about our abilities and inabilities: an internalized stability whereby we measure ourselves versus our own standards and not against the standards of someone else. My fame in the eyes of others doesn't matter; my sense of myself does.[13]

An American illustration comes from the inventor and statesman Benjamin Franklin (1706–90) who was forced to confront his own lack of humility as a young man. We start with a wisecrack of his that you could easily find on the internet: "Even if I could conceive that I had completely overcome [pride], I should probably be proud of my humility." Funny— and yes, this is indeed a genuine quote—typical Franklin, cutting and witty. But it's not a meme that mocks humility, as it's commonly and incorrectly presented; instead, it's a sentiment that endorses the virtue.

Writing when he was seventy-nine years old, Franklin tells us in his autobiography that in his youth he'd listed a dozen virtues he wanted to pursue in his attempt to attain moral perfection. A Quaker friend noted Franklin's frequent expressions of pride and didn't hold back, informing him that in fact he could be overbearing, arrogant, and downright rude when someone tried to demonstrate that he was wrong. In response, Franklin relates, he thought about his friend's candid observation, which made him add humility as the thirteenth goal on his list along with an exercise: "Imitate Jesus and Socrates."

Now read the paragraphs before that punchline and you realize that, placed in context, it's not a punchline at all. His Quaker friend had scored a point. Franklin reports that as a result of that conversation he stopped using words of certainty and tried to draw back from believing himself right and others wrong all the time.

> I even forbid myself . . . the use of every word or expression in the language that imported a fix'd opinion, such as *certainly, undoubtedly*, etc., and I adopted, instead of them, *I conceive, I apprehend,* or *I imagine* a thing to be so or so; or it *so appears to me at present.* When another asserted something that I thought an error, I deny'd myself the pleasure of contradicting him abruptly, and of showing immediately some absurdity in his proposition; and in answering I began by observing that in certain cases or circumstances his opinion would be right, but in the present case there *appear'd* or *seem'd* to me some difference, etc.

What happened when he adopted a humbler approach to the opinions of others?

> I soon found the advantage of this change in my manner; the conversations I engag'd in went on more pleasantly. The modest way in which I propos'd my opinions procur'd them a readier reception and less contradiction; I had less mortification when I was found to be in the wrong, and I more easily prevail'd with others to give up their mistakes and join with me when I happened to be in the right.

Take another look at that alleged punchline as the closing sentence of this episode in his life from the autobiography.

> In reality, there is, perhaps, no one of our natural passions so hard to subdue as *pride*. Disguise it, struggle with it, beat it down, stifle it, mortify it as much as one pleases, it is still alive, and will every now and then peep out and show itself; you will see it, perhaps, often in this history; for, even if I could conceive that I had completely overcome it, I should probably be proud of my humility.

So, in fact, Franklin isn't writing a quip at all, even if the quote does show up on Instagram and Facebook as if it is. He really did learn the hard way that he was arrogant and needed to work at being humble. Though he deliberately acted humbly often so it became a habit, he sometimes struggled to practice what he preached. In a 1755 letter, he advised, "Those who affect to be thought to know everything, and so undertake to explain everything, often remain long ignorant of many things, that others could and would instruct them in, if they appeared less conceited." He was continually learning the lesson of being humble.[14]

   Some stood up to warn against the consequences of forgetting about humility. Romanticism was a nineteenth-century artistic and literary movement that reacted against the hubris of the scientific revolution, the hyper-rationalist tendencies of the Enlightenment, and the social results of the Industrial Revolution. Prince Albert's declaration represents just the kind of historical arrogance, not humility, that Romanticism resisted. Romantic artists and authors feared the factory system was dehumanizing workers and machinery was destroying nature. They weren't against progress, but they cried for limitations, valuing emotions over reason alone and calling for a return to the countryside to stem urban expansion that produced awful living conditions. They valued the individual because they feared she'd been lost in the factory system. They also valued nature, which was directly opposed to Prince Albert's sense of things, because they saw nature as bigger than human creation and beyond human control. To make their point, Romantic artists painted unpopulated or sparsely populated landscapes. In the United States, there's the Hudson River School, with painters such as Thomas Cole (1801–48), whose work appears on this book's cover, and Frederic Edwin Church (1826–1900) in Europe, Romantic painters included Caspar David Friedrich (1774–1840), J. M. W. Turner (1775–1851), and John Constable (1776–1837). Their paintings depict not only nature but sometimes ruins of medieval castles, abbeys, or Roman temples, to remind us of lost glory—buildings put up by people who were sure they were the center of the universe too.[15]

There are certainly many early modern examples of hubris forgetting humility in historical events and fiction. We'll start with an important literary call for caution from the Romantic reaction, Mary Wollstonecraft Shelley's *Frankenstein; or, the Modern Prometheus*, first published in 1818. As Shelley recounted in her preface to the 1831 edition, the idea for the novel came to her when she was nineteen in a writing contest for scariest story with Lord Byron, another friend, and her husband, Percy Bysshe Shelley, in a villa on Lake Geneva. It was a rainy summer, so they spent dreary days inside reading ghost stories and talking about the latest scientific developments. Her idea came to her while she dozed: a horrifying flash of an image of a man bringing a dead creature to life and then being terrified by the work of his own hands. Her novel contrasts science with symbols of uncontrolled nature: uncultivated landscapes, macabre and supernatural settings, and fantastic events.

Frankenstein is not the creature, as later Hollywood movies good and bad implied, but the name of the creator, Dr. Victor

Frankenstein. A restless Victor had studied at the University
of Ingolstadt. He is taken with a particular lecture by Professor
Waldman voicing the scientific revolution's spirit of inquiring
minds: "They penetrate into the recesses of nature, and show
how she works in her hiding places. They ascend into the
heavens; they have discovered how the blood circulates, and
the nature of the air we breathe. They have acquired new and
almost unlimited powers; they can command the thunders of
heaven, mimic the earthquake, and even mock the invisible
world with its own shadows." Victor is smitten. He wants to
play God. As he tells us:

> No one can conceive the variety of feelings which bore me
> onwards, like a hurricane, in the first enthusiasm of success.
> Life and death appeared to me ideal bounds, which I should
> first break through, and pour a torrent of light into our dark
> world. A new species would bless me as its creator and
> source; many happy and excellent natures would owe their
> being to me. No father could claim the gratitude of his child
> so completely as I should deserve theirs. Pursuing these
> reflections, I thought, that if I could bestow animation upon
> lifeless matter, I might in process of time (although I now
> found it impossible) renew life where death had apparently
> devoted the body to corruption.

Frankenstein's creature is smart and huge, but also ugly and
lonely. Expecting to feel jubilation, the creator is horrified by
the line he has crossed, just as in Shelley's dozing dream. Victor sees his mistake in wanting to control the life force: "I had
desired it with an ardour that far exceeded moderation."

More than a creepy tale, the novel is a commentary on
the scientific revolution, with Victor standing in for the arrogance of unchecked science. The subtitle referring to him
as the modern Prometheus links Victor to the Greco-Roman

mythological figure who stole fire from the gods and handed over to mortals this life-giving but potentially destructive element. Zeus severely punished Prometheus for the theft: an eagle eats his liver over and over again as the organ continually grows back. Shelley's morality tale is less about the creature than the creator who loses control of the body he'd animated. In the end, Victor is a broken man who realizes the fault is his: "Learn from me, if not by my precepts, at least by my example, how dangerous is the acquirement of knowledge, and how much happier that man is who believes his native town to be the world, than he who aspires to become greater than his nature will allow." It was hubris that brought Victor down, hubris that killed his family, and hubris that destroyed him. The creature made and abandoned by the creator ended up ruining the creator, but the fault lies not in the hands of the creature as much as in the conscience of the arrogant creator.[16]

Forgetting Humility's Consequences

We can nod at this fictional example and too confidently (arrogantly?) dismiss it. That's them, not us. We'd never be that greedy, naive, or stupid. We have perspective, a conscience, savvy. Once we think that, we've already crossed a line. Consider a 1956 letter in which the Southern Gothic author Flannery O'Connor (1925–64) identified the great Catholic sin as smugness, adding "I find it in myself and don't dislike it any less."[17] That brutally honest one-word self-indictment— smugness—applies all too well and frequently to many modern people and events despite our sense that we advanced far beyond ancient and medieval mumbo jumbo. We confidently live in a scientific age of reason, but hubris did bring us down in times some can still remember.

How did that happen? It's complicated, but a huge contributing factor to twentieth-century conflicts are the ideologies of nationalism and imperialism. Nationalism is full of pros and cons. There's nothing wrong with being proud of your nation, geography, language, customs, folklore, dress, music, dance, and the arts. They provide us with a sense of proper pride and perspective; awareness of heritage can make us humble, grateful, and determined to share our culture. We feel that we belong to a community and hold ideals that are bigger than ourselves. Some of the work of the Romantics tapped into what the Germans call *Volksgeist* or the national spirit of a people. It can lead people to recover their past by gathering and digitizing objects, texts, and records for the future. Nationalism, properly understood and embraced, can even create humility, by placing us in a long history and demonstrating that we aren't the culmination of civilization but rather stewards of a culture for a time.

But there's often not much humility in nationalistic sentiment, which is typically based in nostalgia instead of historical facts understood in context. It's frequently deployed by a ruling group against other groups within one nation and between nationalities. Political scientist Benedict Anderson offered a helpful phrase, calling a nation an "imagined community." Deployed negatively, nationalism is a way of keeping certain groups—based typically on race, ethnicity, or religion—out of power within a country's dominant imagined community. In the nineteenth-century United States, some WASPs (White Anglo-Saxon Protestants) didn't think Jews or Irish and Italian Catholics could ever be good Americans. Outside the Middle East, Africa, and Indonesia, Muslims today sometimes find that they are distrusted even after becoming citizens of the nations to which they have immigrated. French right-wing supporters cry out, "La France pour les Français!" ("France for the French!"), which declares clearly that there is a group, "the French," that has already been identified. Others need not apply.[18]

When national pride goes too far, it becomes arrogant: "We first" morphs into "them second," which might mean kicking people who don't look like "us" and so are "them" out of the country. Popular or cultural nationalism is joyful; political and authoritarian nationalism is destructive. Patriotism is fine; rabid jingoism and xenophobia aren't. Rooting for your country in the Olympics or World Cup is fun; booing the other team isn't. Humiliating another group may make you feel better, but it's hubris at its worst. That hubris led to war and genocide during much of the twentieth century.

In the nineteenth and twentieth centuries, nationalism fueled and was in turn fed by imperialism in a deadly combination. Imperialism is grounded in an unequal relationship: the government officials of the imperial power act from the presumption that they are superior to the conquered. Then they turn these people into colonists below them. This sense of superiority justifies their taking over the land, exploiting what is claimed to be a partnership, and trying to remake the indigenous population and culture in the imperialists' image.

Think of the sheer condescension in the racist poetry of Rudyard Kipling (1865–1936). Referring to Filipinos as captives in "The White Man's Burden" (1899), he praises the great sacrifices American imperialists must suffer to serve the needs of

> Your new-caught sullen peoples,
> Half devil and half child.

Be ready to be stymied by those ungrateful lesser peoples, Kipling warns:

> And when your goal is nearest
> The end for others sought,
> Watch Sloth and heathen Folly
> Bring all your hopes to nought.

The imperialists must be ready to check their pride and to accept

> The blame of those ye better
> The hate of those ye guard.

In Kipling's "Gunga Din" (1890), an Indian servant is mistreated and insulted by the British yet dies saving one of them. The last line is meant to acknowledge his worth, "You're a better man than I am, Gunga Din," but the British held him up as a good Indian because he served them to his death. He had no value outside his deference to their authority. A 1939 movie presents Gunga Din's great ambition to be a British soldier. In the last scene, what looks like his spirit floats over his dead body as it's carried through the British camp. In the overlaid image, Din stands proudly in a British uniform, smartly saluting and smiling. Bagpipes and drums play the Scottish song "Auld Lang Syne."[19]

The worst example of hubris and its destructive power in the twentieth century belongs to Nazism. Has there ever been a leader so narcissistic as Hitler, who destroyed himself and his entire country in a fever dream of supposed superiority? His delusional arrogance convinced others to collaborate with him in declaring his Aryan race purer than any other. Lesser beings didn't deserve to have what they had, so the only option was to purify Germany, then the rest of Europe, of people the Nazis declared to be outsiders: Jews, Roma, those with mental and physical disabilities, anyone who wasn't heterosexual, and many other groups labeled "less-than" in the degrading ancient sense. Hitler told disaffected World War I veterans, a middle class stymied by uncontrolled inflation, failed professionals, bankrupt business owners, and student flunkies like himself that nothing was their fault. Their greatness was unappreciated and needed to be uncovered. Nothing should or could stop them. The glue was all based in hubris: raging nationalism, antisemitism, anti-Communism, and social Darwinism. Using books, games, toys, songs, and summer camps, he brainwashed and indoctrinated children into relying entirely on his Nazi system: Hitler Youth for boys, Faith and Beauty for girls.

In the end, Hitler was brought down by his hubris. Certain that he was the greatest leader who had ever lived, he turned out to be a lousy military commander. He promised his Third Reich would flourish for a thousand years like ancient Rome; it lasted little more than a decade. Resistant to bad news, he ignored facts that didn't fit his irrational scenario. He knew it all and was left with nothing—and then was too much of a coward to face defeat, so he killed himself and abandoned all those followers who'd pledged to never abandon him. All for ego. All for pride. All for arrogance. All for hubris.

Remembering

Is it any wonder, then, that people started to remember humility? Part of the reason why has to be what World War II did to us. People had trusted too much in their own wits. They relied on their technology and what they thought was progress—both technically and morally. They saw what happened when a monster like Hitler seduced millions of self-righteous followers into thinking they were so perfect that others who weren't like them shouldn't even be allowed to live. The United States dropped onto Japanese cities two atomic bombs so powerful no country has dropped them again. Once more: an example of frightening technological advancement, but what about moral progress? Nuclear war is an effective way to kill many people at once. Should we be proud or humbled by that action? Just what is progress? Had we become chastened like Prometheus? Like ancient Athens waking up after losing to Sparta, modern people asked: Now what?

Not everyone had forgotten humility entirely: think of Mary Shelley and Immanuel Kant. But the breathless pace of change shoved humility aside. You can't deny how fast things accelerated in the twentieth century. Some people who read a newspaper to learn about the Wright brothers' flights in 1903 watched on live TV when human beings walked on the moon just sixty-six years later. At the same time, as we've seen, not all developments can be called progress. Systematically and efficiently transporting Jews on cattle cars, separating those who were too weak to work from those who could, and eventually killing them all in gas chambers and burning their bodies in crematoria was the Nazis' sick idea of technical and societal progress, but it certainly wasn't a moral advance. So one thing that occurred in the last century was a growing sense that our world today is not the best or the be-all and end-all of human civilization and history—a hard lesson to learn.

To start talking about how we began to re-embrace humility, let's tackle an attitude called the tyranny of chronology that not just the Nazis displayed. I'm alive today, other cultures fell, but things are great for me so my place and time must be superior. My life, and so the world, revolves around my smartphone. Right here, right now, all is for the best in the best of all possible worlds, as Voltaire's characters kept inanely declaring in the face of one misfortune and disaster after another in his satirical novel *Candide* (1759).

The main characters Candide, his tutor Pangloss, and their friend Cunégonde are battered by slavery, rape, physical assault and combat, shipwreck, an earthquake, and almost being eaten by cannibals. Nevertheless, and almost bizarrely, Pangloss spins everything as further proof that theirs is the best of all possible worlds. For instance, the syphilis that took one of Pangloss's eyes and ears was a result of encounters between Columbus's men and the indigenous people they encountered, but the Europeans also brought chocolate back to Europe, so it was all for the best. In reality, the three traveled throughout Europe, South America, the Middle East, and back again only to find themselves after all their learning, wealth, and adventures on a small farm. Voltaire demonstrates that Candide's insatiable desire for more-more-more (even El Dorado didn't satisfy him) only made him realize in the end that living simply on that farm might be humbler and better than Pangloss's hubris of achievement and progress. To the very end of the play, Pangloss is still trying to convince Candide otherwise:

> "There is a concatenation of events in this best of all possible worlds: for if you had not been kicked out of a magnificent castle for love of Miss Cunégonde: if you had not been put into the Inquisition: if you had not walked over America: if you had not stabbed the Baron: if you had not lost all your sheep from the fine country of El Dorado: you would not be here eating preserved citrons and pistachio-nuts."
>
> "All that is very well," answered Candide, "but let us cultivate our garden."

In the end, Candide had seen it all, done it all—and was exhausted and emptied by it all. He realized that humbler was better.[20]

Another brake on naive modern optimism and the tyranny of chronology comes from the middle of the nineteenth century, from a Swiss historian of culture named Jacob Burckhardt (1818–97). Thinking philosophically, he gave a lecture "On the Fortune and Misfortune in History" at the Museum of Basel in 1871. There he considered self-obsession, which is what we saw Pangloss displaying when he placed himself and his friends at the center of history. Everything culminates in us: today and in this place. Burckhardt scoffed at this notion: "Just as if the world and its history had existed merely for our sakes! For everyone regards all times as fulfilled in his own, and cannot see his own as one of many passing waves."[21]

In a similar way, C. S. Lewis (1898–1963), a medieval literature professor better known for his Chronicles of Narnia, starting with *The Lion, the Witch, and the Wardrobe,* was quite open about the lessons he had to learn about not putting himself in the center of place and time. He recounts that a college friend of his from Oxford, Owen Barfield, "made short work of what I have called my 'chronological snobbery,' the uncritical acceptance of the intellectual climate common to our own age and the assumption that whatever has gone out of date is on that account discredited." Was an idea just a fad or trend that lived its life and passed away to be replaced by the next shiny thing? Was it discredited by a better idea? Do we discount the Roman empire's achievements because it didn't last more than five hundred years, and they're gone but we're here? Lewis learned the lesson Pangloss hadn't: "From seeing this, one passes to the realization that our own age is also 'a period,' and certainly has, like all periods, its own characteristic illusions. They are likeliest to lurk in those widespread assumptions which are so ingrained in the age that no one dares to attack or feels it necessary to defend them."[22]

Apart from these reflections in a memoir, Lewis also offered lessons on humility in a charming, imagined correspondence between Screwtape, a senior devil in hell, and his nephew Wormwood, an apprentice who has just been assigned his first soul (called the patient) to corrupt. In letter 14 of the *Screwtape Letters,* which he published in the middle of 1942 when there wasn't a lot of humility going around, Lewis has Screwtape (who refers to God as the Enemy) play with the temptation of being proud of humility:

Your patient has become humble; have you drawn his attention to the fact? . . . Catch him at the moment when he is really poor in spirit and smuggle into his mind the gratifying reflection, "By jove! I'm being humble," and almost immediately pride—pride at his own humility—will appear. If he awakes to the danger and tries to smother this new form of pride, make him proud of his attempt.

The problem seems to be that Wormwood's patient is enjoying the fruits of humility, which has turned his self-absorption into a concern for others. This fact makes Screwtape ring the alarm bell and recommend the ancient strand of humiliation.

You must therefore conceal from the patient the true end of Humility. Let him think of it not as self-forgetfulness but as a certain kind of opinion (namely, a low opinion) of his own talents and character. Some talents, I gather, he really has. Fix in his mind the idea that humility consists in trying to believe those talents to be less valuable than he believes them to be.

For Screwtape, the worst outcome would be for the patient to actually understand humility in the way we've been tracking: proper pride in his accomplishments, a sense of what he can and can't do, and appreciation for what others have achieved. He gives an example: the patient could design the most beautiful cathedral of the world and be no more or less proud of his skill than if someone else had done the same thing. "The Enemy wants him, in the end, to be so free of any bias in his own favor that he can rejoice in his own talents as frankly and gratefully as in his neighbor's talents—or in a sunrise, an elephant, or a waterfall."[23]

A Humbled Institution

Just as individuals can be proud and arrogant, so too can nations, communities, institutions, companies, and schools. We've all experienced the arrogance of power, frequently in the guise of people claiming knowledge is power—and they're not sharing the knowledge. There's the school principal who says she's in control of a hazing allegation or a threat of school violence but won't release details of the investigation. Presidents of universities and companies might impose ethical training and standards on employees but don't follow the rules themselves because they think they're above the law. A board of trustees or directors wants to see full transparency in employees in charge of allocated funds but refuses to agree to a forensic audit when allegations of executive financial impropriety arise. Groups have mission statements, but when leaders don't apply them equally and fairly, the whistleblower and not the violator takes the heat. Asked hard questions, the authorities often take offense: how dare we question their authority, which is a bizarre response for public officials elected to serve the common good and to represent their constituents. They are above; we are below. They say they know better, which makes us ask: Who's guarding the guards?

If it's hard for an individual to learn humility, it's even harder for an institution. One example we might explore is Roman Catholicism in light of the sex abuse scandals that, while known in some circles and kept quiet, exploded in January 2002 with a *Boston Globe* exposé that was depicted in the 2015 film *Spotlight*. That investigation was followed by others across the globe documenting decades of sexual abuse by priest-pedophiles, most of which had been covered up by bishops who chose to transfer those priests to other parishes where they might harm again rather than turn them into civil authorities. Worldwide Catholicism took a massive credibility hit.

Part of the problem was the arrogance of the pedophiles, who as priests enjoyed a certain societal deference that protected them, and of the bishops who thought their decisions were outside the law. So the Catholic Church was both humiliated for the crimes and cover-ups as well as humbled because it lost much of its prestige and authority.

A number of theologians and church historians took this event as a moment of self-reflection and saw the humbling of the church as a very good thing. Self-righteousness had been taken down several notches; bishops and priests were revealed to have been saying one thing but hypocritically doing quite another. While preaching that all were equal in God's eyes, it became clear that priest-pedophiles were excused and protected while survivors were victimized not only by their sexual abusers but again by the institutional church in not being believed, in being belittled, and in being manipulated to keep quiet "for the good of the church" so that there would not be scandal or damage to "Father's reputation." In trying to avoid one scandal and be sure they could always control the narrative, some church leaders created another scandal that was their own fault. Is it any wonder why the church suffered such a self-inflicted crisis of its authority and credibility? Once more, hubris had conquered humility.

What's next? Can these leaders learn humility? Margaret A. Farley, a prominent ethicist, used a helpful phrase to describe the humble attitude that chastened church leaders should embrace: the grace of self-doubt. There is a good that comes from stopping to ask: Am I right? Were my actions correct? Could I have done better? She believed this attitude could counter priestly authoritarianism—the imposed obedience, threatening tone, and false certainty. Building on Farley's concept of a humbling grace of self-doubt, Paul Lakeland, a leading theologian, declared that the problem lay in the church's hubris and the notion that it was an exclusive club that could keep others out even by protecting criminals within. But now was a teachable moment: humiliation could lead to humility if church leaders realized that they needed help. Without humility, church leaders would continue to engage in a monologue and cast down edicts rather than have a dialogue in which they owned up to the impact of their failures.[24]

Summarizing over a decade of self-reflection, humiliation, and growing humility, the theologian Richard R. Gaillardetz put the events since 2002 in a longer context, reaching back to the early 1960s and the worldwide Catholic council known as Vatican II. What had the church learned in the bumpy and unsettling half-century since then? Gaillardetz observed that the church's sense of itself, viewed through the prism of humility, could be quite a positive development. After the *Boston Globe* reports, some (but not all or nearly enough) church leaders had undertaken a process of personal and institutional self-assessment and recognized the need for reform and renewal. By embracing Vatican II's image of the church as a pilgrim—on the way, with good intentions, but not there yet—he saw the merit of a church that was honest enough with itself to admit past errors.[25]

Will the church truly embrace humility? The jury is still out. Yet a shocking exercise of humility occurred within Catholicism in recent memory. On February 11, 2013, Pope Benedict XVI declared he would resign at the end of that month, ending his papacy, which had begun in 2005. He was the consummate company man who at times wielded his power with a heavy hand, an Old World courtier with a taste for elaborate vestments. Benedict seemed like the last person to display his own frailty openly. But he was quite honest and forthcoming in the announcement: he simply realized, after taking a hard look at himself, that at the age of eight-five he was no longer up to the job physically or emotionally.[26] Few knew a pope *could* resign. There had been just a handful in history. The most famous was Celestine V, who quickly understood that he'd been a bad choice for pope and stepped down after less than six months in office in 1294 for the same reasons Benedict listed. The Italian poet Dante Alighieri in his *Inferno* assigned Celestine V a spot just inside the gate of hell for his "great refusal" *(il gran rifiuto)* of the papal office due to cowardice. Dante reserved this place at hell's doorstep for those who lived without praise or blame.[27]

Benedict's act was astounding, if not entirely unprecedented. Still, as the last pope to resign since Gregory XII in 1415, Benedict's stepping down was striking. In a world of power, who walks away? From a political standpoint, the papacy is the longest-lasting monarchy in world history. From a religious standpoint, the pope is the vicar or representative of Jesus on earth. Who would abandon that post and give up that authority? The answer is someone who realized, for all of his achievements and missteps, for all of his successes and failures, that the office of the papacy is bigger than the person who holds it. In stepping down as pope, Benedict XVI demonstrated that humility is still a virtue.

Notes

1. Of the many books about Teresa, two that place her particularly well in time, place, and cultural contexts are Bilinkoff, *Ávila of St. Teresa*; and Ahlgren, *Teresa of Ávila*.

2. Teresa of Ávila, *Interior Castle*, 42–44 (First Dwelling Places, I.2.8–11). On these points, see Fullam, "Teresa of Avila's Liberative Humility," 175–98, and Sawall, "Teresa of Avila," 109–19.

3. Ignatius of Loyola, *A Pilgrim's Testament*, 4–14, 31–50, 79 (sections 1–12, 19–37, 54); de Dalmases, *Ignatius of Loyola*, 24–48, 54–70, 85–89.

4. Ignatius of Loyola, *Ignatius of Loyola*, 263–64; Young, "Spiritual Journal of Ignatius Loyola," 243.

5. Ignatius of Loyola, *Spiritual Exercises*, 72–73 (Second Week, paragraphs 165–67).

6. Calvin, *Institutes of the Christian Religion*, 923 (3.21.2).

7. Bynum, "Wonder," 1–26.

8. Darwin, *On the Origin of Species*, 10.

9. Hume, *Treatise*, 186–97 (II.I.2–7); Hume, *Enquiry*, 73 (9.1); Hume, *Dialogues*, 163 (Natural History, X).

10. For a discussion of the extent to which Hume represented his age, see Davie, "Hume on Monkish Virtues," which tries to soften Hume's absolutism against humility; Button, "'A Monkish Kind of Virtue,'" 840–68, which counters the notion that Hume was entirely against humility, especially in the context of what he identifies as "ethnic and cultural pluralism"; and Reed, "What's Wrong with Monkish Virtues?" 39–56, which argues that Hume reflects the conventional beliefs of his time.

11. For the complete speech, see Black et al., *Broadview Anthology*, vol. 5, 1223–24.

12. Kant, *Metaphysics of Morals*, 201–2 (Part I, Book I, Chapter II, Part III), original emphasis.

13. Grenberg, *Kant and the Ethics of Humility*, 93, 141–62.

14. Franklin, *Autobiography of Benjamin Franklin*, 65–74, original emphasis, with the letter at 138–39n59; Isaacson, *Benjamin Franklin*, 89–92.

15. Though not part of the Atlantic world's Romantic movement, another contemporary painter with the same feel is Japanese artist Katsushika Hokusai (1760–1849). He was painting in the tradition of Japanese landscapes where nature is the star and humans or animals, if present, stand small and humble before its grandeur. One of his classics is the blue and white *Under the Wave off Kanagawa*, also called *The Great Wave*, that he painted about 1830–32. So fierce is the wave that you might miss the three boats about to be crushed, which is likely one of his points.

16. There are many editions of Mary Shelley's *Frankenstein*; the episodes here are from chapters 3–5, 7, 16–17, 20–23.

17. O'Connor, *Habit of Being*, 131.

18. Anderson, *Imagined Communities*.

19. Kipling, *Collected Verse*, 215–17, 271–74.

20. There are many editions of Voltaire's *Candide*; the episodes here are from chapters 4, 17–20, 30.

21. Burckhardt, *Force and Freedom*, 358.

22. Lewis, *Surprised by Joy*, 207–8.

23. Lewis, *The Screwtape Letters*, 67–70.

24. Farley, "Ethics, Ecclesiology, and the Grace of Self-Doubt," 66–70; Lakeland, "'I Want To Be in That Number,'" 16–28; Paul Lakeland, "Reflections on the 'Grace of Self-Doubt,'" in Doyle et al., *Ecclesiology and Exclusion*, 13–17; and Lakeland, *Council That Will Never End*, 101–54. On monologue versus dialogue, see Gerard Mannion, "Response: Ecclesiology and the Humility of God: Embracing the Risk of Loving the World," in Doyle et al., *Ecclesiology and Exclusion*, 24–41.

25. Gaillardetz, "Vatican II," 87–108.

26. For an account of his decision and aftermath, see Benedict XVI and Seewald, *Last Testament in His Own Words*, 15–26; and O'Connell, *Election of Pope Francis*, 3–15.

27. Dante, *Divine Comedy*, "Inferno," canto 3, 1–60.

EPILOGUE

Recovering a Lost Virtue

> Arrogance leaves us blind to our own weaknesses. Humility is a reflective lens: it helps us see them clearly. Confident humility is a corrective lens: it enables us to overcome those weaknesses.
> *Adam Grant, 2021*

As we come to the end of this inquiry into humility, it's helpful to gather together some lessons and legacies of the lost virtue so we can start recovering it. We face a challenge at the outset: many still see humility as a vice embracing the ancient notion of humiliation. There's a great deal of distrust of people trying to look humble when they really aren't. There are also justifiable cautions against people abusing humility because they might be deploying the idea to defend their own authority and demand obedience, as Teresa of Ávila had warned.

Humility Is a Healthy Attitude of Perspective and Proportion

How to begin to recover the lost virtue? Think of humility as a base or center point, the hub of a wheel out of which other virtues radiate. This is why Hildegard of Bingen called humility the queen of the virtues and wrote that the other virtues don't know what to do without her. Other ways to describe the key role of humility are to think of this virtue as a disposition, a fundamental or foundational stance, or a posture. Certainly the negative conceptions of humility as humiliation, low self-esteem, or timidity can't help us develop personally and professionally in positive ways.

As a healthy state of mind, humility provides perspective and proportion, which was one of Aquinas's insights. In late medieval Paris, Jean Gerson had identified discretion as humility's daughter. Discretion allows us to have a broader view, which fights against the tyranny of chronology, Pangloss's dopey naïveté in *Candide*, or what C. S. Lewis recognized as his own chronological snobbery. Studying any topic, in this case the development of humility, from a long perspective prompts us to realize that everything has a history.[1]

Discretion, perspective, and proportion fight against tribalism, which is in essence group hubris placing my ethnic group, race, nationality, religion, profession, or some other identity marker above other people's. What we gain is Jean Gerson's discerning mind. Being humble forces us to ask, "Where do I fit—in my family or at work? How does my viewpoint stand up to others? Why is my country outstanding—or is it? Why do I need to brag? How can my field work with other professions? Why do I think my values are the only ones that count?"

Humility Makes Us Vulnerable and Grateful

Why would anyone want to feel vulnerable? It's so unmodern, un-individualistic, undesirable. We see vulnerability as a weakness and self-sufficiency as the goal. Recognizing that we're not self-sufficient is humility built on realism. We don't delude ourselves with pretension, ego, or conceit. We realize nobody can go it alone. It's an attitude that can only lead to improvement and expansion, maybe even a path to forgiveness and reconciliation in a broken relationship where we're too proud to say, "I'm sorry." Humility starts with "Something's off here. I'll go first with what I think is my fault." Because of this entry point, you're more likely to have that conversation with restraint and respect. It just may be that your friend, coworker, even your opponent or enemy might be right.

Being humble and vulnerable means you're more likely to be listening, not talking at someone. You're conversing, not telling. You understand that your information and opinion might be incomplete or shaded by factors you can't see because they are so ingrained. That means that your conclusions might be undermined by a weak link, which is why Descartes insisted in his long chains of reasoning that you don't proceed until you are sure you've considered all factors. He started not with certainty, which is arrogant and foolish, but skepticism, which is wise and a good strategy.

A healthy skepticism reveals where you need help. You might have to trust someone else. By being self-aware, you become self-reflective. Then and only then can we accept blame and fix our flaws with aid from someone to whom you'll naturally be grateful—either for teaching you something new or stopping you from making an ass of yourself.

Humility Promotes Moderation

Humility is an example of the moderation that's been lost in public discourse. This virtue forces us away from extreme, fundamentalist, and ideological positions. Humility reminds us that we might not be right all the time.

Today's civil discourse isn't so civil. Moderation is no longer praised. Extreme wings frequently set the agenda for faiths and political parties: both sides are always yelling. For some, political affiliation is based on faith, not principle or fact. Aligning with a particular political party, interest group, or identity plays out like religious zeal with speeches that sound like sermons, songs and slogans that sound like hymns, and symbols wielded like sacraments. The marketplace of ideas has become a zero-sum game: I have to win and you have to lose. We're extreming ourselves to death.

Humility can help us see the gray between my black-and-white and someone else's black-and-white. Stepping back from this fervor is the first step in finding not the differences but a middle ground based on fairness, equity, and justice for all. Humble moderation slows conversations down, gives closed minds and cold hearts a chance to pause, and can build consensus. Humility and moderation can force us to look at our own prejudices, biases, stereotyping, sprints to condemnation, and a desire for total victory. We can find that other ideas and needs have merit, too, even if we may not like them. We don't have to agree totally, but a political conversation that takes the best options from among several competing ideas and avoids their worst elements can help build a more perfect union.

Moderation can bring peace even when there is not full agreement between two people in families, workplaces, or among nations. The virtue of moderation that grows from humility is specifically helpful in countries where many different groups live in the same space. This is especially the case in the early twenty-first century, as swaggering patriotism and hyped-up xenophobia around the globe threaten democracies and toleration.

Extremism seems to dominate—or at least fringe elements get more media coverage and more financial backing, which could well create tyrannies of minorities that feel threatened and so lash out. Such groups seem to be happy to triumph, even if it means burning their entire systems and their own communities down around them. They don't want to yield to compromise and coexistence, good ways of getting things done for the common good that are now dismissed as signs of weakness. The arrogant tail of extremism is wagging the dog of humble moderation. In that case, we all lose.

In an odd twist, being a moderate has become a radical position. Pause for a moment to draw from Aristotle a word of praise for moderation as a virtue sitting in the middle road like humility. Some criticize moderates with the easy bark that they're just walking a cowardly yellow line down the middle of the road. "Take a stand, dammit!" they say. "This is no time for half-measures. If you're not with us, you're against us." Most of us have experienced coworkers or relatives who go from one extreme to the other. The left-wing hippie becomes the buttoned-down conservative. The atheist becomes a believer and promptly tells longtime members of their new faith tradition where they've lost their way. The overweight person who's slimmed down counts not only the calories on his plate but on ours too. Being an extremist or acting with the convert's fire may make you a zealot or a sieve, but humbly maintaining balance is much harder.

Speaking moderately doesn't mean being without conviction. The moderate must speak firmly to both sides. The challenge is to confront a policy or person without being confrontational. Moderates of many faiths and political parties fight extremists within their own tradition—insiders who fear their faith is being hijacked by fanatics and radicals, violent in their words or deeds, who don't speak the truth of their religious or political principles but get the most attention. Extremists happily wash out subtlety and boil their traditions down to silly slogans. There is no humility in extremism. Moderates embrace flaws to find a better way for a greater number of people. Like humility, its fruit of moderation is still a virtue if only we have the courage to practice it.

Humility Can Restore a Sense of Community

Humility produces dialogue, not a monologue. I have to listen. Shutting up allows me to hear things that might help. A humble outlook demonstrates that we're not self-sufficient as individuals or as members of any one identity group. There is a social compact of mutual obligation. The common good matters. It's the glue of civil society around the world, even as we watch that society becoming increasingly uncivil—which illustrates the need for more humble interdependence.

This is an ancient insight: Confucius warned against individuality that puts one person above many. In his tradition, the duties of mutual obligations placed the community ahead of the individual, and these duties promoted cooperation. Filial piety, respect for elders, and brotherly love formed an umbrella. Individuals were interlocked in a tapestry woven from five key relationships: in government between rulers and the ruled, between spouses, between parents and their children, among siblings, and within circles of friendship.[2]

In the modern world, dependence might have been seen as a weakness instead of a good trait that recognized the need for us to help each other. Independence can be overvalued when it leads to the notion that being a lone wolf is a prize. Philosopher Alasdair MacIntyre took up this challenge of pushing back against rabid independence in *After Virtue*, published in 1981. There, he reconsidered the idea of a healthy community in a context of (as he saw it) rampant relativism and individuality. MacIntyre praised the enduring debt that modernity owed to the community-centered aspects of Greco-Roman and medieval European societies even as he was accused of nostalgia, as he noted in a later edition in 2007. MacIntyre identified contemporary culture's divorce from that debt and warned that we separated ourselves from that tradition's sense of community at our peril.[3]

Another call for humble interaction, interdependence, and community thinking came from Barbara Jordan (1936–96), the first Black woman elected to the House of Representatives from the South and the first Black Texan to serve in Congress. Invited to give the 1976 Democratic National Convention keynote, she chose to spend part of her speech on the relationship between the individual and the community. Jordan saw civil society endangered by selfishness on the part of individuals and groups competing with each other for power and domination:

> Many fear the future. Many are distrustful of their leaders, and believe that their voices are never heard. Many seek only to satisfy their private work—wants; to satisfy their private interests. But this is the great danger America faces—that we will cease to be one nation and become instead a collection of interest groups: city against suburb, region against region, individual against individual; each seeking to satisfy private wants. If that happens, who then will speak for America? Who then will speak for the common good?

Jordan offered an alternative that implicitly presented a benefit of humility: the sense that we need each other.

> Are we to be one people bound together by common spirit, sharing in a common endeavor; or will we become a divided nation? . . . We must address and master the future together. It can be done if we restore the belief that we share a sense of national community, that we share a common national endeavor. It can be done.

How could that happen in a decade full of distrust of government and the fierce retreat to our own sidelines that often comes from fear—as she put it, a time "when self-interest and bitterness seem to prevail"? Jordan's answer was a shared, and we would add *humble*, sense of the benefits for all in seeking the common good. We're either in this together or we're not. The first way helps; the second way destroys.[4]

Humility Can Fight Stubbornness

Humble doubt is OK. Proud certainty is dangerous. Charles Darwin had a sense of this insight. In his introduction to *The Descent of Man* (1871), published about a decade after *On the Origin of Species*, in which he'd presented his work as conditional and not definitive, he strongly asserts: "ignorance more frequently begets confidence than does knowledge: it is those who know little, and not those who know much, who so positively assert that this or that problem will never be solved by science."[5] We've all lived with this: the boorish person who hasn't held down a job in years, fails in one relationship after another, blames everyone else for his problems, is clueless, never looks in a mirror—and yet somehow is sure he's an expert on everything who just has to tell you why you're stupid and get fooled all the time.

Lacking humility makes you dig in and double down because admitting you're mistaken is seen as humiliating. Willful people impose their views on others. They badger and bulldoze in place of persuading and discussing. They don't care about your feelings but cry if you offend theirs. The more insecure and uninformed they are, the louder and more bullying they act. They fail to be open to the chance that they might be misinformed, mistaken, or—worst of all for their needy egos—not the center of everyone else's universe.

Humility allows you to back down from that stubbornness and from absolute stances. You can admit error: "I realize I was in the wrong. I'll act differently now." A responsible citizen is an informed citizen. That means listening to all parties, becoming fully informed, and then making judicious decisions instead of only grabbing on to the parts of the story that support my self-serving and often ideological preconceptions. That's the precise opposite of learned ignorance.

By choosing to be humble, we're choosing to be upset,

disturbed, confronted; we're starting with the premise that there's more we don't know. That attitude makes it easier to make a course correction while also promoting persistent curiosity. Humility helps us restore the idea that there is yet something to be learned from somebody else. It gives you an out. That very interaction is a step toward building community with a shared sense of purpose in righting wrongs instead of winning.

Humility Can Be Learned

Are we born humble? Maybe. But if not, can we learn to be humble? If the answer is no, then we're in trouble. But the history of humility says the answer is yes. We can learn to be humble, or at least a bit humbler, than we are now.

We often say that we want our children to grow up confident and resilient. Humility is a virtue that helps with both of those goals. As organizational psychologist Adam Grant said: confident humility is the next logical step once we recognize our weaknesses. Having honestly evaluated ourselves, we can set out to improve our shortcomings. Ian James Kidd, a philosopher interested in his field's application to real-world situations, agrees. By practicing humility, we can come to a right balance reminiscent of Aristotle and Confucius. "Concisely, then," he writes, "humility is a virtue for the management of confidence." That kind of confidence is good pride and not hubris, a positive virtue and not a vice that makes a person overblown, arrogant, demeaning of others, self-serving, and self-absorbed.[6]

Without humility, the arrogance and dictatorship of power will inevitably threaten our lives and stability—and cause the death of shame. We've witnessed leaders in our families, jobs, schools, neighborhoods, and governments at the local, state, and national levels with no shame. We've come to learn that some people will never do the right thing. Why? Because they have no humility. Without humility, there can be no honor. Never expect honor from people without shame. Don't expect empathy from such people either. That empathy gap is a serious hole in our communities today. It's robbed us of our humanity.

What are we to do? Learn to be humble, that's what. Aristotle said that we are what we repeatedly do. We build character with practice that develops habit. We've learned to watch what people do more than to listen to what they say. Words are cheap. Actions are hard. The latter reveal character. Oprah Winfrey recounts learning a hard lesson about this from the great American voice Maya Angelou. She sagely taught that when a person shows you who they are, believe them the first time.[7]

Some people cannot learn because they have no desire to be taught—and why? Because they don't think that anyone can tell them anything. I'm reminded of a lesson that a choir director shared: never try to teach a pig how to sing. It wastes your time and annoys the pig. Desire is the first step. Those willing to learn are already on the way, just like the women who knocked on the door of Hildegard of Bingen's or Teresa of Ávila's convents without really understanding what was inside. Benedict of Nursia in the sixth century and Ignatius Loyola in the sixteenth laid steps to pursue humility.

In our own time, an openness to humility can be cultivated early, starting when our children are young. Little ones have an admirable open-mindedness that our cynicism buries as we age; we need to fight that tendency. They can learn to evaluate themselves positively in sports and clubs; on a wider scale, kids can learn humility by experiencing other neighborhoods, schools, and states, and if possible other nations, on family trips or study abroad programs.

Youth is the time of life when habits are more easily grounded, but anyone who has quit smoking knows that you can replace a bad habit with a good habit at any age.

Encountering others with an open mind to our own skills and limitations is instructive. We can practice gratitude for the opinions, experiences, and generosity of other people and groups. We can examine our own culture of ranking and labeling people by wondering how people rank and label us. When we see someone else's talents and skills, are we envious or admiring? It's fine to be properly proud of our own talents and skills (I can teach a good course) as well as properly humble when understanding our own deficiencies or inabilities in manual things (I can't change the oil in my car). We can't fix a flaw that we don't admit exists.[8]

We've seen in this history of humility examples where humility has been misunderstood and misused along with admirable insights from philosophers and painters, theologians and ethicists, historians and novelists, playwrights and politicians. We pursued the development of humility by exploring its treatments in Greco-Roman history, philosophy, and literature; ancient and medieval Jewish, Christian, and Muslim traditions; and Enlightenment and contemporary discussions on education in virtue and citizenship.

The history of humility has demonstrated that when the virtue of humility is cast aside, hubris follows. But we have also found, in evidence dating back to ancient Greece and China, that humility balances and moderates us. The medieval golden age taught us that learned ignorance is quite a helpful perspective on the path to humility. We saw in modernity how the ancient periods' twin strands of humility competed. A battered twentieth century began to tip the scale back to the value of humility as an attractive and worthy character trait for individuals, groups, and nations.

We've seen what happens without humility. When hubris triumphs, everyone loses. What we found is that humility is a lost virtue that's worth recovering.

Humility's time has come again.

Notes

1. Norvin Richards, a philosopher interested in applied ethics, particularly explores perspective and proportion as products of a humble stance in *Humility*, 1–20.
2. Confucius, *Li Ki*, 313; this book came to be separated out from the *Classic of Rites* as the *Doctrine of the Mean*.
3. MacIntyre, *After Virtue*, xi, 121–203.
4. Barbara Jordan, "1976 Democratic National Convention Keynote Address." Congressional Record 122 (July 27, 1976), p. E24127–28. On some of Jordan's points related to how political communities form or don't, see Carter, *Integrity* and *Civility*. For a longer historical lens and evaluation, see Davetian, *Civility*.
5. Darwin, *Descent of Man*, 3.
6. Grant, *Think Again*, 54; Kidd, "Educating for Intellectual Humility," 57. For examples relating the learning of humility to the traditional hero's journey, see Worthington and Allison, *Heroic Humility*.
7. Oprah Winfrey, "When People Show You Who They Are, Believe Them," Oprah.com, October 26, 2011, recalling a 1997 conversation, https://www.oprah.com/oprahs-lifeclass/when-people -show-you-who-they-are-believe-them-video.
8. Baehr, *Inquiring Mind*, 140–62; Roberts, "Learning Intellectual Humility," 184–201; and Whitcomb et al., "Intellectual Humility," 509–39. For a discussion of intellectual modesty and a critique on the dangers of false modesty, see Tanesini, "Intellectual Humility as Attitude," 399–420.

BIBLIOGRAPHY

Abelard, Peter. *Ethical Writings*. Translated by Paul Vincent Spade. Indianapolis: Hackett, 1995.

———. *Peter Abailard: Sic et Non, A Critical Edition*. Edited by Blanche B. Boyer and Richard McKeon. Chicago: University of Chicago Press, 1977.

Abelard, Peter, and Heloise. *The Letters of Abelard and Heloise*. Rev. ed. Translated by Betty Radice. London: Penguin, 2003.

Abu Sway, Mustafa. "Islamic Theological Perspectives on Intellectual Humility and the Conditioning of Interfaith Dialogue." In *Learned Ignorance: Intellectual Humility among Jews, Christians, and Muslims*, edited by James L. Heft and Omid Safi, 225–37. Oxford: Oxford University Press, 2011.

Ahlgren, Gillian T. W. *Teresa of Ávila and the Politics of Sanctity*. Ithaca, NY: Cornell University Press, 1998.

Alfano, Mark, Michael P. Lynch, and Alessandra Tanesini, eds. *The Routledge Handbook of Philosophy of Humility*. London: Routledge, 2021.

Al-Ghazālī. *The Faith and Practice of Al-Ghazālī*. Translated by W. Montgomery Watt. London: George Allen and Unwin, 1953.

Anderson, Benedict. *Imagined Communities: Reflections on the Origin and Spread of Nationalism*. 2nd ed. London: Verso, 2006.

Anderson, C. Colt. "Recovering the Apologetics of Humility." *New Theology Review* 23 (2010): 25–33.

Andrews, Frances. *The Early Humiliati*. Cambridge: Cambridge University Press, 1999.

Appiah, Kwame Anthony. *The Honor Code: How Moral Revolutions Happen*. New York: Norton, 2010.

Aquinas, Thomas. *Summa Theologica*. 5 vols. Westminster, MD: Christian Classics, 1948.

Aristotle. *Aristotle's Nicomachean Ethics*. Translated by Robert C.

Bartlett and Susan D. Collins. Chicago: University of Chicago Press, 2011.

Augustine. *Confessions*. Translated by R. S. Pine-Coffin. New York: Penguin Classics, 2015.

———. *Homilies on the Gospel of John 1–40*. Translated by Edmund Hill. Hyde Park, NY: New City Press, 2009.

———. *Selected Writings*. Translated by Mary T. Clark. New York: Paulist Press, 1984.

Austin, Amy M., and Mark D. Johnston, eds. *A Companion to Ramon Llull and Lullism*. Leiden: Brill, 2019.

Baehr, Jason. *The Inquiring Mind: On Intellectual Virtues and Virtue Epistemology*. Oxford: Oxford University Press, 2011.

Bejczy, István. *The Cardinal Virtues in the Middle Ages: A Study in Moral Thought from the Fourth to the Fourteenth Century*. Leiden: Brill, 2011.

Bejczy, István, and Richard G. Newhauser, eds. *Virtue and Ethics in the Twelfth Century*. Leiden: Brill, 2005.

Bell, Rudolph M. *Holy Anorexia*. Chicago: University of Chicago Press, 1985.

Benedict XVI, and Peter Seewald. *Last Testament in His Own Words*. Translated by Jacob Phillips. London: Bloomsbury, 2016.

Bernard of Clairvaux. *The Steps of Humility and Pride*. Translated by Ambrose Conway. Kalamazoo, MI: Cistercian, 1989.

Bilinkoff, Jodi. *The Ávila of St. Teresa: Religious Reform in a Sixteenth-Century City*. Ithaca, NY: Cornell University Press, 2015.

Black, Joseph, Leonard Conolly, Kate Flint, Isobel Grundy, Don LePan, Roy Liuzza, Jerome J. McGann, Anne Lake Prescott, Jason Rudy, Barry V. Qualls, and Claire Walters, eds. *The Broadview Anthology of British Literature*. Vol. 5, *The Victorian Era*. 3rd ed. Peterborough, Ontario: Broadview Press, 2021.

Boland, Paschal. "The Concept of Discretio Spirituum in John Gerson's 'De probatione spirituum' and 'De distinctione verarum visionum a falsis.'" PhD dissertation, Catholic University of America, 1959.

Brasher, Sally Mayall. *Women of the Humiliati: A Lay Religious Order in Medieval Civic Life*. New York: Routledge, 2003.

Brown, Raymond E. *An Introduction to the New Testament*. New York: Doubleday, 1997.

Brown, Raymond E., Joseph A. Fitzmyer, and Roland E. Murphy, eds. *The New Jerome Biblical Commentary*. Upper Saddle River, NJ: Prentice Hall, 1990.

Burckhardt, Jacob. *Force and Freedom: Reflections on History*. Edited by James Hastings Nichols. New York: Pantheon, 1943.

Burrows, Mark S. *Jean Gerson and De Consolatione Theologiae (1418): The Consolation of a Biblical and Reforming Theology for a Disordered Age*. Tübingen: J. C. B. Mohr (Paul Siebeck), 1991.

Button, Mark. "'A Monkish Kind of Virtue'? For and against Humility." *Political Theory* 33 (2005): 840–68.

Bynum, Caroline Walker. *Holy Feast and Holy Fast: The Religious Significance of Food to Medieval Women*. Berkeley: University of California Press, 1987.

———. "Wonder." *American Historical Review* 102 (1997): 1–26.

Calvin, John. *Institutes of the Christian Religion*. Vol. 1. Edited by John T. McNeill. Translated by Ford Lewis Battles. Louisville, KY: Westminster John Knox Press, 2006.

Carter, Stephen L. *Civility: Manners, Morals, and the Etiquette of Democracy*. New York: Basic, 1998.

———. *Integrity*. New York: Basic, 1996.

Casey, Michael. *A Guide to Living in the Truth: Saint Benedict's Teachings on Humility*. Liguori: Liguori/Triumph, 2001.

Catherine of Siena. *The Dialogue*. Translated by Suzanne Noffke. New York: Paulist Press, 1980.

Chadwick, Owen, ed. *Western Asceticism*. Philadelphia: Westminster, 1958.

Chenu, Marie-Dominique. *Nature, Man, and Society in the Twelfth Century*. Edited and translated by Jerome Taylor and Lester K. Little. Chicago: University of Chicago Press, 1968.

Chittister, Joan. *The Rule of Benedict: Insights for the Ages*. New York: Crossroad, 1992.

———. *Wisdom Distilled from the Daily: Living the Rule of St. Benedict Today*. New York: HarperOne, 1990.

Confucius. *Analects: With Selections from Traditional Commentaries*. Translated by Edward Slingerland. Cambridge, MA: Hackett, 2003.

———. *The Li Ki*. In *The Sacred Books of China: The Texts of Confucianism*, translated by James Legge. London: Clarendon, 1885.

Corcoran, Donald. "Benedictine Humility and Confucian 'Sincerity.'"

In *Purity of Heart and Contemplation: A Monastic Dialogue Between Christian and Asian Traditions*, edited by Bruno Barnhart and Joseph Wong, 227–41. London: Continuum, 2001.

Dante. *The Divine Comedy*. Translated by Burton Raffel. Evanston, IL: Northwestern University Press, 2010.

Darwin, Charles. *The Descent of Man, and Selection in Relation to Sex*. Princeton: Princeton University Press, 1981.

———. *On the Origin of Species*. New York: Appleton, 1861.

Davetian, Benet. *Civility: A Cultural History*. Toronto: University of Toronto Press, 2009.

Davie, William. "Hume on Monkish Virtues." *Hume Studies* 25 (1999): 139–53.

Dawes, S. B. "ANAWA in Translation and Tradition." *Vetus Testamentum* 41 (1991): 38–48.

———. "Humility: Whence This Strange Notion?" *Expository Times* 103 (1991): 72–75.

de Dalmases, Cándido. *Ignatius of Loyola, Founder of the Jesuits: His Life and Work*. Translated by Jerome Aixalá. St. Louis: Institute of Jesuit Sources, 1985.

Demacopoulos, George A. *Gregory the Great: Ascetic, Pastor, and First Man of Rome*. Notre Dame, IN: University of Notre Dame Press, 2015.

de Voragine, Jacobus. *The Golden Legend: Readings on the Saints*. Translated by William Granger Ryan. Princeton: Princeton University Press, 1993.

Dickson, John P., and Brian S. Rosner. "Humility as a Social Virtue in the Hebrew Bible?" *Vetus Testamentum* 54 (2004): 459–79.

Dickson, Gary. "Encounters in Medieval Revivalism: Monks, Friars, and Popular Enthusiasts." *Church History* 68 (1999): 265–93.

———. "The Flagellants of 1260 and the Crusades." *Journal of Medieval History* 15 (1989): 227–67.

Diodorus Siculus. *Library of History*. Vol. 4. Translated by C. H. Oldfather. Cambridge: Harvard University Press, 1946.

Doyle, Dennis D., Timothy J. Furry, and Pascal D. Bazzell, eds. *Ecclesiology and Exclusion*. New York: Orbis, 2012.

Dronke, Peter. *Poetic Individuality in the Middle Ages: New Departures in Poetry, 1000–1150*. Oxford: Clarendon, 1970.

Dubbelman, Samuel J. "I Know That I Do Not Know: Nicholas of Cusa's Augustine." *Harvard Theological Review* 113 (2020): 460–82.

Epstein, I., ed. and trans. *The Babylonian Talmud. Seder Mo'ed.* London: Soncino Press, 1938.

Farley, Margaret A. "Ethics, Ecclesiology, and the Grace of Self-Doubt." In *A Call to Fidelity*, edited by James J. Walter, Timothy E. O'Connell, and Thomas A. Shannon, 5–75. Washington, DC: Georgetown University Press, 2002.

Franklin, Benjamin. *The Autobiography of Benjamin Franklin.* Edited by Peter Conn. Philadelphia: University of Pennsylvania Press, 2005.

Fullam, Lisa. "Teresa of Avila's Liberative Humility." *Journal of Moral Theology* 3 (2014): 175–98.

Gaillardetz, Richard R. "Vatican II and the Humility of the Church." In *The Legacy of Vatican II*, edited by Massimo Faggioli and Andrea Vicini, 87–108. New York: Paulist Press, 2015.

Gerson, Jean. *De distinctione verarum visionem a falsis*, in *Oeuvres complètes*, 11 vols. in 10, edited by Palemon Glorieux, 3:36–56. Paris: Desclée, 1960–73.

Glick, Thomas F. "'My Master, the Jew': Observations on Interfaith Scholarly Interaction in the Middle Ages." In *Jews, Muslims, and Christians in and around the Crown of Aragon*, edited by Harvey J. Hames, 157–82. Leiden: Brill, 2004.

Goodman, Philip. *The Yom Kippur Anthology.* Philadelphia: Jewish Publication Society of America, 1971.

Grant, Adam. *Think Again: The Power of Knowing What You Don't Know.* New York: Viking, 2021.

Green, Ronald. "Jewish Ethics and the Virtue of Humility." *Journal of Religious Ethics* 1 (1973): 53–63.

Gregory the Great. *Homilies on the Book of the Prophet Ezekiel.* 2nd ed. Translated by Theodosia Tomkinson. Etna, CA: Center for Traditionalist Orthodox Studies, 2008.

———. *Moral Reflections on the Book of Job.* Vol. 5. Translated by Brian Kerns. Collegeville, MN: Cistercian/Liturgical Press, 2019.

Grenberg, Jeanine. *Kant and the Ethics of Humility.* Cambridge: Cambridge University Press, 2005.

Groppe, Elizabeth. "After Augustine: Humility and the Search for

God in Historical Memory." In *Learned Ignorance: Intellectual Humility among Jews, Christians, and Muslims*, edited by James L. Heft and Omid Safi, 191–209. Oxford: Oxford University Press, 2011.

Habig, Marion A., ed. *St. Francis of Assisi. Writings and Early Biographies*. Chicago: Franciscan Herald Press, 1973.

Hall, David L., and Roger T. Ames. *Thinking through Confucius*. Albany: SUNY Press, 1987.

Hildegard of Bingen. *Scivias*. Translated by Columba Hart and Jane Bishop. New York: Paulist Press, 1990.

Hinze, Bradford E. "Ecclesial Repentance and the Demands of Dialogue." *Theological Studies* 61 (2000): 207–38.

Horace and Persius. *Satires and Epistles of Horace and Persius*. Translated by Niall Rudd. London: Penguin Classics, 2005.

Hume, David. *Dialogues concerning Natural Religion and the Natural History of Religion*. Edited by J. C. A. Gaskin. Oxford: Oxford University Press, 1998.

———. *An Enquiry Concerning the Principles of Morals*. Edited by Tom L. Beauchamp. Oxford: Clarendon, 1998.

———. *A Treatise of Human Nature*. Edited by John P. Wright, Robert Stecker, and Gary Fuller. London: Everyman, 2003.

Ignatius of Loyola. *Ignatius of Loyola: Spiritual Exercises and Selected Works*. Edited by George E. Ganss. New York: Paulist Press, 1991.

———. *A Pilgrim's Testament*. Translated by Parmananda R. Divarkar. Saint Louis: Institute of Jesuit Sources, 1995.

———. *The Spiritual Exercises of St. Ignatius: A Translation and Commentary*. Translated by George E. Ganss. Saint Louis: Institute of Jesuit Sources, 1992.

Isaacson, Walter. *Benjamin Franklin: An American Life*. New York: Simon and Schuster, 2003.

Iversen, Gunilla. "*Ego Humilitatis, Regina Virtutum*: Poetic Language and Literary Structure in Hildegard of Bingen's Vision of the Virtues." In *Ordo Virtutum of Hildegard von Bingen: Critical Studies*, ed. Audrey Ekdahl Davidson, 79–110. Kalamazoo, MI: Medieval Institute, 1992.

Jalabi, Afra. "Walking on Divine Edge: Reading Notions of Arrogance and Humility in the *Qur'an*." In *Learned Ignorance: Intellectual Humility among Jews, Christians, and Muslims*, edited by James L. Heft and Omid Safi, 170–88. Oxford: Oxford University Press, 2011.

Johnson, Elizabeth A. *Truly Our Sister: A Theology of Mary in the Communion of Saints.* New York: Continuum, 2003.

Jordan, Barbara. "1976 Democratic National Convention Keynote Address." *Congressional Record* 122 (July 27, 1976): E24127–28.

Kardong, Terrence G. "The Heights of Humility." *Studia Monastica* 38 (1996): 26–67.

Kamali, Mohammad Hashim. *The Middle Path of Moderation in Islam: The Qur'anic Principle of Wasatiyyah.* Oxford: Oxford University Press, 2015.

Kant, Immanuel. *The Metaphysics of Morals.* Edited by Lara Denis. Translated by Mary Gregor. Cambridge: Cambridge University Press, 2017.

Keenan, James F. *Moral Wisdom: Lessons and Texts from the Catholic Tradition.* Lanham, MD: Rowman and Littlefield, 2004.

Kidd, Ian James. "Educating for Intellectual Humility." In *Intellectual Virtues and Education: Essays in Applied Virtue Epistemology*, edited by Jason Baehr, 54–70. New York: Routledge, 2016.

Kipling, Rudyard. *Collected Verse of Rudyard Kipling.* Garden City, NY: Doubleday, 1920.

Lakeland, Paul. *A Council That Will Never End: Lumen Gentium and the Church Today.* Collegeville, MN: Liturgical Press, 2013.

———. "'I Want to Be in That Number': Desire, Inclusivity, and the Church." *Catholic Theological Society of America Proceedings* 66 (2011): 16–28.

Latteur, Emmanuel. "The Twelve Degrees of Humility in St. Benedict's *Rule*: Still Timely?" *American Benedictine Review* 40 (1989): 32–51.

Leclercq, Jean. "The Renewal of Theology." In *Renaissance and Renewal in the Twelfth Century*, edited by Robert L. Benson and Giles Constable, with Carol D. Lanham, 68–87. Toronto: University of Toronto Press, 1991.

Lehmijoki-Gardner, Maiju. "Denial as Action—Penance and Its Place in the Life of Catherine of Siena." In *A Companion to Catherine of Siena*, edited by Carolyn Muessig, George Ferzoco, and Beverly Mayne Kienzle, 113–26. Leiden: Brill, 2012.

Lewis, C. S. *The Screwtape Letters.* London: Geoffrey Bles, 1961.

———. *Surprised by Joy.* New York: Harcourt Brace Jovanovich, 1955.

Louf, André. *The Way of Humility*. Translated by Lawrence S. Cunningham. Kalamazoo, MI: Cistercian, 2007.

MacIntyre, Alasdair. *After Virtue*. 3rd ed. Notre Dame: University of Notre Dame Press, 2007.

Macqueen, D. J. "Augustine on *Superbia*: The Historical Background and Sources of His Doctrine." *Mélanges de Science Religieuse* 34 (1977): 193–211.

McGinn, Bernard. *The Doctors of the Church*. New York: Crossroad, 1999.

———. "Seeing and Not Seeing: Nicholas of Cusa's *De visione Dei* in the History of Western Mysticism." In *Cusanus: The Legacy of Learned Ignorance*, edited by Peter Casarella, 26–53. Washington, DC: Catholic University of America Press, 2006.

McGuire, Brian Patrick. *Jean Gerson and the Last Medieval Reformation*. University Park: Pennsylvania State University Press, 2005.

———. trans. *Jean Gerson: Early Works*. New York: Paulist Press, 1998.

McInerney, Joseph J. *The Greatness of Humility: St. Augustine on Moral Excellence*. Eugene, OR: Pickwick, 2016.

McNeill, John T., and Helena M. Gamer, trans. *Medieval Handbooks of Penance*. New York: Columbia University Press, 1990.

McPherson, Kirstin Carlson. "The Secular Transformation of Pride and Humility in the Moral Philosophy of David Hume." PhD dissertation, Marquette University, 2016.

Mohamed, Yasien. "The Duties of the Teacher: Al-Iṣfahānī's *Dharī'a* as a Source of Inspiration for al-Ghazālī's *Mīzān al-'Amal*." In *Islam and Rationality*, vol. 1, edited by Georges Tamer, 186–206. Leiden: Brill, 2015.

Moorhead, John. *Gregory the Great*. London: Routledge, 2005.

Myers, David G. "The Psychology of Humility." In *God, Science and Humility: Ten Scientists Consider Humility Theology*, edited by Robert L. Herrmann, 153–75. Radnor, PA: Templeton Foundation Press, 2000.

Neil, Bronwen, and Matthew Dal Santo, eds. *A Companion to Gregory the Great*. Leiden: Brill, 2013.

Nicholas of Cusa. *On Learned Ignorance*. 2nd ed. Translated by Jasper Hopkins. Minneapolis: Arthur J. Banning, 1985.

O'Connell, Gerard. *The Election of Pope Francis: An Inside Account of the Conclave That Changed History*. New York: Orbis, 2019.

O'Connor, Flannery. *The Habit of Being: Letters of Flannery O'Connor*. Edited by Sally Fitzgerald. New York: Farrar, Straus and Giroux, 1979.

Pardue, Stephen T. *The Mind of Christ: Humility and the Intellect in Early Christian Theology*. London: Bloomsbury, 2013.

Pascoe, Louis B. *Jean Gerson: Principles of Church Reform*. Leiden: Brill, 1973.

Petersen, Joan M., trans. *Handmaids of the Lord: Contemporary Descriptions of Feminine Asceticism in the First Six Christian Centuries*. Kalamazoo, MI: Cistercian, 1996.

Plato. *The Last Days of Socrates*. Translated by Hugh Tredennick and Harold Tarrant. London: Penguin, 2003.

Ramsey, Boniface, trans. *John Cassian: The Institutes*. New York: Newman, 2000.

Reed, Philip A. "What's Wrong with Monkish Virtues?" *History of Philosophy Quarterly* 29 (2012): 39–56.

Resnick, Irven M., ed. *A Companion to Albert the Great*. Leiden: Brill, 2013.

Richards, Norvin. *Humility*. Philadelphia: Temple University Press, 1992.

Richardson, Cyril C., ed. *Early Christian Fathers*. New York: Touchstone, 1996.

Roberts, Robert C. "Learning Intellectual Humility." In *Intellectual Virtues and Education: Essays in Applied Virtue Epistemology*, edited by Jason Baehr, 184–201. New York: Routledge, 2016.

Rushing, Sara. "What Is Confucian Humility?" In *Virtue Ethics and Confucianism*, edited by Stephen C. Angle and Michael Slote, 173–81. New York: Routledge, 2013.

Sawall, Marina. "Teresa of Avila and the Relationship of Humility to Insight." *Studies in Spirituality* 29 (2019): 109–19.

Schaff, Philip, ed. *A Select Library of the Nicene and Post-Nicene Fathers*. Vol. 1. Grand Rapids, MI: Eerdmans, 1956.

Seneca. *Moral Letters to Lucilius*. Vol. 2. Translated by Richard Mott Gummere. London: W. Heinemann, 1920.

Sherman, Nancy. *Stoic Wisdom: Ancient Lessons for Modern Resilience*. Oxford: Oxford University Press, 2021.

Sommerfeldt, John R. *The Spiritual Teachings of Bernard of Clairvaux.* Kalamazoo, MI: Cistercian, 1991.

Stoudt, Debra, George Ferzoco, and Beverly Mayne Kienzle, eds. *A Companion to Hildegard of Bingen.* Leiden: Brill, 2013.

Straw, Carole. *Gregory the Great: Perfection in Imperfection.* Berkeley: University of California Press, 1988.

Sutera, Judith, trans. *St. Benedict's Rule: An Inclusive Translation.* Collegeville, MN: Liturgical Press, 2021.

Swan, Laura. *The Forgotten Desert Mothers: Sayings, Lives, and Stories of Early Christian Women.* New York: Paulist Press, 2001.

Tanesini, Alessandra. "Intellectual Humility as Attitude." *Philosophy and Phenomenological Research* 96 (2018): 399–420.

Templeton, John. *The Humble Approach: Scientists Discover God.* Philadelphia: Templeton Foundation Press, 1998.

Teresa of Ávila. *The Interior Castle.* Translated by Kieran Kavanaugh and Otilio Rodriguez. New York: Paulist Press, 1979.

Thucydides. *History of the Peloponnesian War.* Translated by Rex Warner. New York: Penguin, 1972.

Trinkaus, Charles. *In Our Image and Likeness: Humanity and Divinity in Italian Humanist Thoughts.* 2 vols. Chicago: University of Chicago Press, 1970.

Van Tongeren, Daryl R., Don E. Davis, Joshua N. Hook, and Charlotte vanOyen-Witvliet. "Humility." *Current Directions in Psychological Science* 28 (2019): 463–68.

Verbeek, Theo. "From Learned Ignorance to Skepticism: Descartes and Calvinist Orthodoxy." In *Skepticism and Irreligion in the Seventeenth and Eighteenth Centuries,* edited by Richard H. Popkin and Arjo J. Vanderjagt, 31–45. Leiden: Brill, 1993.

Wengst, Klaus. *Humility: Solidarity of the Humiliated.* Translated by John Bowden. Philadelphia: Fortress Press, 1988.

Whitcomb, Dennis, Heather Battaly, Jason Baehr, and Daniel Howard-Snyder. "Intellectual Humility: Owning Our Limitations." *Philosophy and Phenomenological Research* 94 (2017): 509–39.

Wielenberg, Erik J. "Secular Humility." In *Humility,* edited by Jennifer Cole Wright, 41–63. Oxford: Oxford University Press, 2019.

———. *Value and Virtue in a Godless Universe.* Cambridge: Cambridge University Press, 2005.

Wilkerson, Isabel. *Caste: The Origins of Our Discontent*. New York: Random House, 2020.

Worthington, Everett L., Jr., and Scott T. Allison. *Heroic Humility: What the Science of Humility Can Say to People Raised on Self-Focus*. Washington, DC: American Psychological Association, 2018.

―――. *Humility: The Quiet Virtue*. Philadelphia: Templeton Foundation Press, 2007.

Worthington, Everett L., Jr., Don E. Davis, and Joshua N. Hook, eds. *Handbook of Humility: Theory, Research, and Applications*. New York: Routledge, 2017.

Wright, Jennifer Cole. "Humility as a Foundational Virtue." In *Humility*, edited by Jennifer Cole Wright, 146–74. Oxford: Oxford University Press, 2019.

Young, William J., trans. "Spiritual Journal of Ignatius Loyola." *Woodstock Letters* 87 (1958): 195–267.

INDEX

ABOUT THE AUTHOR

Dr. Christopher M. Bellitto is professor of history at Kean University in New Jersey, where he teaches courses in ancient and medieval history. With a focus on church history and reform, he has twice won grants from the National Endowment for the Humanities. He has been a visiting scholar at Princeton Theological Seminary and a Fulbright specialist at the University of Canterbury in New Zealand and the University of Groningen in the Netherlands. Dr. Bellitto serves as series editor in chief of Brill's Companions to the Christian Tradition and academic editor at large for Paulist Press. He also frequently offers public lectures and comments in the media on church history and contemporary Catholicism.